DATE DUE

~~JE 1 0 '02~~			
~~AG 8 '02~~			
~~AG 8 '02~~			
~~DE 21 '02~~			
~~FE 20 '03~~			
~~MAY 2 4 2006~~			

DEMCO 38-296

Images of
Mainstreaming

SOURCE BOOKS ON EDUCATION
VOLUME 53
GARLAND REFERENCE LIBRARY OF SOCIAL SCIENCE
VOLUME 1145

Images of Mainstreaming
Educating Students with Disabilities

Edited by
Robert McNergney and Clayton Keller

Garland Publishing, Inc.
A member of the Taylor & Francis Group
New York and London
1999

Library of Congress Cataloging-in-Publication Data

Images of mainstreaming : educating students with disabilities / edited by
  Robert McNergney and Clayton Keller.
        p.   cm. — (Garland reference library of social science ; vol. 1145.
Source books on education ; vol. 53)
    Includes bibliographical references (p.) and index.
    ISBN 0-8153-2593-2 (alk. paper)
    1. Handicapped children—Education (Elementary)—United States—Case
studies.   2. Mainstreaming in education—United States—Case studies.
3. Special education teachers—United States—Case studies.   I. McNergney,
Robert F.   II. Keller, Clayton E.   III. Series: Garland reference library of social
science ; v. 1145.   IV. Series: Garland reference library of social science.
Source books on education ; vol. 53.
LC4031.I49   1999
371.9'046'0973—dc21   98–46764
                                                                        CIP

Printed on acid-free, 250-year-life paper
Manufactured in the United States of America

To the memory of our friend and colleague,
Mary Catherine Ellwein

Contents

FIGURES

Acknowledgments

We speak for the other members of the research team in thanking the following agencies for their generous assistance during the course of the project. Much of our work was supported by Grant No. G008630227 from the Office of Special Education Research, U.S. Department of Education. We also received support from the Curry School of Education and the State Council of Higher Education for Virginia. The Virginia State Education Department helped with some of the data analyses.

We owe thanks to many individuals. The project would have collapsed on several occasions without the crucial assistance of Chandlee Bryan, Denise Huffman, John Lloyd, Margaret Wood, Marion Rabinowitz, Sterling Deal, Renita Parrish, Karen Dwier, Peggy Marshall, Sandy Davis, Phillis Palmore, and Gail Duggan. We thank Michael Spurlock, our editor at Garland Publishing Inc., for demonstrating faith in our work. We also thank our good colleagues at The Hitachi Foundation for stretching our thinking about case-method teaching and learning. Most of all we are indebted to the administrators, teachers, parents, and students of Charter Hills.

RFM and CEK

Preface

We have written this book to describe a set of studies conducted on teaching students with learning disabilities who were mainstreamed in elementary schools. As we explain in Chapter 1, the studies, both quantitative and qualitative, examined the thinking and behavior of more and less effective teachers. We report results of investigations of students' actions in some of the classrooms we observed. We have tried to place our work in the present sociopolitical context of mainstreaming to avoid fixating on methodological details at the expense of thinking about the real, practical problems of teaching children with special needs in regular classrooms.

We have included a chapter by Mary Catherine Ellwein (see Chapter 8) in which she reflected on earlier drafts of the cases included in this volume. She died before the project was completed, but Mary Catherine helped shape our thinking about the value of listening to teachers in their own words.

We have written mainly for teachers, teacher educators, education researchers, and education policymakers. On the one hand, it may seem that we have erred on the side of providing too much detail. On the other, we might be faulted for being too terse. These are judgment calls, and we are to be blamed if the manuscript swings too far in either direction.

Images of
Mainstreaming

CHAPTER 1

Teacher Thinking and Behavior in Mainstreamed Classrooms

Robert F. McNergney, Daniel P. Hallahan, and
Joanne M. Herbert
University of Virginia

When the typical American public school teacher looks out across the faces of her[1] or his 25 to 30 students approximately 2 to 4 of the students looking back have disabilities. In addition, there are usually at least 2 to 4 other children with learning and behavioral difficulties who are at risk of formal identification. Teaching these children in regular or general education classrooms—"mainstreaming" students, as it has come to be called—is a fact of life in schools throughout the land. For teachers the challenge is one of helping all their students succeed. But how are teachers to create opportunities for all their students to succeed?

In this chapter we explain how we have tried to answer this question and to address the related problem of how teacher educators can help teachers. We describe our overall methodology and explain why we proceeded as we did. Finally, we discuss the sociopolitical context in which we did our work and in which mainstreaming occurs across the country.

THE SETTING, THE AUTHORS, THE TIMES

The studies reported here were conducted in and around the pseudonymous community of Charter Hills, a small city on the eastern seaboard of the United States. At first glance the casual observer on the beaten path might think the citizens' values and wealth are more evenly shared than they are. Indeed, because of the community's place in

American history and its picturesque setting, it often serves as the scene of photo opportunities for politicians, major and minor. Presumably these pictures communicate a wholesomeness and commitment to intellectual vigor important to a person who would represent the people. In fact, like many smaller cities in which a large university is located, Charter Hills is characterized by considerable economic and cultural diversity. These attributes and their influence, however indirect, on life in schools are felt most notably in the case studies and in the synthesis of the cases presented in later chapters.

One of the more useful ways to characterize collectively the authors of the chapters is as a tribe. Over the course of the project, members played different roles. Some gathered data, others sifted these data. Some harvested literature and located people to provide special kinds of insight into particular problems. Still others hunted money to provide sustenance to the group. All shared willingly of their time and thoughts and wrote and rewrote material until it was in a form that we believed represented fairly what occurred and how these events were interpreted. The time that people were able to commit to the project varied. At times each member of the core research team was fully engaged in project work; at other times a different set of duties took precedence for some members of the team. Some people played more than one role. At one time or another everyone, by virtue of his or her knowledge and nerve, served as chief. People left to join other tribes and to take on new tasks.

As we have worked on this project, public education has moved to page one in many local and national newspapers. Following wave after wave of education reform reports, starting with *A Nation at Risk* in 1983, people both inside and outside the education establishment have realized that there were lots of reasons to be interested in the health of elementary and secondary schools.

Presidents Reagan, Bush, and Clinton, governors galore, college presidents, teachers' union presidents, chief executive officers of corporations, and many other national, state, and local officials have made education issues part of our everyday conversation. Most likely every good (and bad) idea ever imagined for reforming public education has surfaced during this period of time.

The country's economy has waxed, waned, and waxed again during this time. The schools in which all of us worked appeared largely unaffected by these conditions until near the end of the project when some layoffs of teachers and administrators occurred. The schools also seemed relatively untouched by the "big educational issues" that have dominated headlines—teacher incompetence, violence in schools, moribund curriculum, and the like. Life has gone on much as it had before all the national attention. That is not to say that people in the school system are impervious to change or that they are unconcerned. Quite the contrary. They have exhibited what most of us think of as an air of professionalism. They have had their jobs to do, and all the talk about education that has swirled around them has not changed that fact.

MAINSTREAMING: PROBLEMS OF PLACEMENT OR PRACTICE?

On a policy level some have argued that mainstreaming is a blueprint for failure—too many needy students, too many ill-prepared teachers, too little support for those teachers who are efficacious in their classroom behavior. For them, the answer is to avoid mainstreaming by placing students with disabilities in self-contained special education classrooms. For still others, the answer is to try to boost the skills of general education teachers so that they can handle whatever problems these "special" children may present.

In the main, policymakers have concerned themselves with issues of placement first and with issues of teaching and teacher education only a distant second. As Edward Zigler (1987) so eloquently observed, policymakers have often mistakenly focused on issues of placement rather than the teaching and learning contexts of those placements:

> We've been spending so much time worrying about retarded people's addresses that we're forgetting about the everyday environments *within* those addresses. I share Urie Bronfenbrenner's concern that we need more than a person's "social address" in order to know about and help that person. (p. 14)

Although Zigler was referring primarily to residential versus community placements for individuals with mental retardation, his comments are apropos for students with mild disabilities who are found in public schools. Once the address is fixed and students with disabilities are placed with typical students in general education classrooms, concerns shift immediately and directly to issues of what goes on in these placements. For purposes of this project, then, we suspended our own opinions of the efficacy of different types of physical placements and concentrated on what went on in one setting, the regular classroom.

How are we to determine what the needs of all students are, and how are we to match instruction to these needs? This compound problem is addressed on a classroom-by-classroom basis by teachers themselves. They must process relevant information and act in ways that maximize chances for student success.

In our work we tried to examine what makes teachers effective in such situations by studying both their behaviors and their thoughts. We tried to understand teachers' thoughts and intentions because we wanted to know more than what good teachers do in mainstreamed classrooms. We also wanted to know why they behave as they do. Indeed, as we note below, research has suggested that both teachers' behaviors and thoughts are important and that when either is viewed independently the observer is likely to form a simplistic impression of classroom life.

UNDERSTANDING TEACHERS' BEHAVIORS AND THOUGHTS

What Mitzel (1960) first characterized as process-product research has yielded a consistently strong set of teaching processes or behaviors associated with students' use of time in classrooms, with their academic achievement, and with their feelings about teaching and learning. As Gage (1985) argued, the knowledge base established via process-product research is much stronger than that which undergirds some so-called miracle cures in the medical sciences. Much of that early research was correlational, making causal connections difficult to claim (Medley, 1977); but later experimental studies demonstrated that when teachers behaved in certain ways they influenced student learning (Brophy & Good, 1986). Based on an analysis of 13 of these experiments, Rosenshine (1983) contended that when students are younger, slower, and/or have little prior knowledge, teachers are most effective when they

> structure the learning; proceed in small steps at brisk pace; give detailed and redundant instructions and explanations; provide many examples; ask a large number of questions and corrections, particularly in the initial stages of learning new material; have a

student success rate of 80% or higher in initial learning; divide
seatwork assignments into smaller assignments; and provide for
continued student practice so that students have a success rate of 90-
100% and become rapid, confident, and firm. (pp. 336-337)

These and similar teaching behaviors have emerged as important
time and again (Gage & Needels, 1989). Walberg's (1984) synthesis of
thousands of research findings led him to conclude that the instructional
processes with the largest positive effects on most students'
performances include reinforcing correct performance, using
instructional cues, encouraging engagement, and providing corrective
feedback. Beyond these factors, Walberg noted the importance of
teachers holding high expectations for student performance and
providing "cognitive maps" that alert students to the planned flow of
instruction.

In Brophy and Good's (1986) definitive summary of process-
product findings, they describe effective teaching in terms of the
quantity and pacing of instruction, grouping strategies, giving
information, questioning students, reacting to student responses, and
handling seatwork and homework assignments. Teachers, Brophy and
Good argue, who

do these things successfully produce significantly more achievement
than those who do not, but doing them successfully demands a blend
of knowledge, energy, motivation, and communication and decision-
making skills that many teachers, let alone ordinary adults do not
possess. (p. 370)

They are also quick to add that such behaviors, if they are to be
understood, must be interpreted in a context that includes attention to
teachers' goals and intentions. "We need to know what teachers are
trying to accomplish in order to interpret their behaviors . . . " (p. 368)

Although much of the process-product research has focused on the
performance of lower-ability students—children who share some
characteristics with special education students being mainstreamed—
there has been relatively little systematic investigation of teaching
behaviors in relation to the performances of students with mild
disabilities who are mainstreamed. Larrivee (1985), however, identified
15 teaching processes that related to several learning outcomes of
mainstreamed students. Her findings suggest that some teachers are

effective with both mainstreamed students and the class as a whole at the same time. It is not clear from Larrivee's work, however, if these effective teachers treated mainstreamed students differently than the other students in the class. It is quite possible that some combinations and frequencies of teaching behaviors are more effective with mainstreamed students and other combinations and frequencies are more effective with typical students.

To rely only on the observable behaviors of teachers, whether in mainstreamed classrooms or in other situations, is to miss important information about success in teaching and learning. Studies of how teachers think, how they make decisions and judgments, and how they solve problems are beginning to narrow the conceptual distance between teachers as people and the professional images they project through their classroom behaviors (Clark & Peterson, 1986). In general, researchers working in this area try to reveal why teachers behave as they do, both in planning for instruction and in interactive situations during the course of teaching. These studies are also, as Clark and Peterson contend, "potential sources of hypotheses about and explanation of some of the puzzling and contradictory findings of process-product research on teaching and of curriculum change implementation research" (p. 292). Efforts to understand what and how teachers think may help school leaders initiate and sustain innovations in ways they have been unable to do in the past.

Jackson (1968; 1990) wrote persuasively about the importance of trying to understand teacher thinking in his classic book *Life in Classrooms*. For him, behavioral observation simply did not reveal what he wanted to know.

> Occupational attitudes, the feelings of satisfaction and of disappointment accompanying success and failure, the reasoning that lies behind action—these and many other aspects of a craft are scarcely visible except through conversations with a person who has experienced them. And it is not only what the practitioner says that is revealing. His way of saying it and even the things he leaves unsaid often contain clues to the nature of his experience. Consequently, talk is necessary, particularly talk about the professional aspects of life in the classroom. (1968, p. 115)

In a sense we used our case studies to reinvent the wheel Jackson designed when teachers taught us about classroom life by talking to us.

In one case, the teacher told us frequently that she did certain things in certain ways because she wanted to boost her students' self-concepts. This fact would not have been evident had we relied merely on behavioral observations of her in the classroom. The intensity with which she held this conviction could only be felt by listening to her talk about her teaching.

Of course simple conceptions of teacher thinking alone, like those of teaching behavior, are unlikely to yield powerful models of practice. As Shulman (1986) noted:

> No single research program can capture the full set of educational events . . . [but] the insufficiencies of particular programs can be overcome through proper blending with the insufficiencies of other programs. This image of a yoking of inadequacies to produce a hybrid more vigorous than either of its parents is certainly not alien to the practice of agriculture, but it has not been widely touted in the social sciences. (pp. 6-7)

Nor do we believe that thought data are always more important or revealing than behavioral data. Using our example above, the fact that the teacher thought she was doing certain things to elevate self-concepts does not necessarily mean that these things were resulting in the desired outcome. What we do believe is that it is more profitable to consider *both* behaviors and thoughts rather than either one in isolation. Furthermore, when discrepancies between thoughts and behavior do occur, they may be important.

In keeping with this view we have tried to use both methods of process-product research and research on teacher thinking to characterize the job of a teacher in a mainstreamed classroom; that is, we have described teachers in terms of what they thought and how they behaved. By asking questions of teachers and tying their thoughts to observable classroom behaviors we began to understand "the immediate and local meanings of actions, as defined from the actors' point[s] of view" (Erickson, 1986, p. 119).

There are several reasons why we think it is worth the time and effort to try to derive such meanings. First, there is broad agreement that one must know what teachers value before any attempt to educate them will succeed. Simply providing rules or prescriptions for teaching will not yield teaching success. As Argyris and Schön (1974) observed, "Nobody else can see for him, and he can't see just by being 'told,'" (p.

151). Second, interest in teachers' thoughts and behaviors conveys to teachers the importance of their role in the improvement of teaching and learning, thus potentially increasing teachers' perceptions of self-efficacy—"an important element of the link between knowledge and behaviors" (Darling-Hammond, Wise, & Pease, 1983, p. 315). Third, teachers can change the way they think about teaching and learning, and ultimately how they behave toward students. But as Peterson (1989) and others have argued, teachers need reasons to change, and these reasons might well be supplied from an understanding that certain classroom actions are both worthwhile and possible.

We began our work with goals in mind. We wanted to describe classroom behavior of more and less effective teachers of mainstreamed students with learning disabilities, to study the behavior and thinking of a few good teachers in depth, and to see if it were possible to encourage other teachers to enrich their thinking and behavior as they interacted with their students.

RESEARCH PROCEDURES

We have used a variety of quantitative and qualitative methods to address our objectives. These have included the use of statistical procedures to cluster data yielded from direct, low-inference observation of teachers and children—observation that requires people to make only minimal judgments about what they see and hear. In interviewing teachers we have looked for their perceptions of what happens in classrooms and why. We have conducted stimulated recall sessions with teachers and students using videotapes of lessons in which they participated to find out what was going through their minds as they interacted with one another. And we have made ecological observations of classrooms in which we have sought to describe as fully and completely as possible what we saw and heard. In all phases of the project we have tried to focus our studies on fourth- or fifth-grade classrooms during the teaching of reading or language arts.

Quantitative Studies

Our quantitative studies have been undertaken to identify more and less effective subtypes of teachers in mainstreamed classrooms by examining their in-class behaviors and relating them to the on-task behavior of their students. We realized at the outset that on-task behavior was not the ideal outcome measure. Information pertaining to achievement, self-concept, and feelings about school, for example, would have been preferable. We thought on-task behavior to be an acceptable dependent variable that would provide us with an indication of student well-being. Using cluster analysis, Clay Keller, Don McKinney, and Joe Sutton analyzed the classroom behaviors of experienced and beginning teachers to yield these subtypes. The subtypes helped guide our early thinking about selecting and analyzing the series of case studies that followed.

Subtype information was based on data collected by observing classrooms directly. We went into classrooms where teachers with typical students and students with disabilities worked together. We used an instrument consisting of some 150 items that we later reduced to 8 groups or factors. Some of these factors were positively related to student involvement and some were negatively related. Teachers in each subtype represent distinctly different profiles on the 8 behavior patterns listed below:

1. Stating expectations—Teacher introduces lesson/activity, begins lesson.

2. Monitoring—Teacher monitors learners/provides assistance and structures learners' responses.

3. Questioning—Teacher asks questions of the group or individual learners.

4. Positive regard—Teacher attempts to motivate individual learners.

5. Negative regard—Teacher ignores individual learners or shows intolerance of behavior.

6. Praising—Teacher praises individual learners.

7. Effective transitions—Teacher prepares learners for a change in activities.

8. Making assignments—Teacher brings lesson to end and makes assignment.

Qualitative Studies

The goal of the qualitative component has been to make explicit what teachers often seem to intuit in teaching students with and without disabilities in general education settings. We have sought to describe in-depth a few teachers from an "inside-out" perspective (Hunt, 1987) by raising to a level of consciousness teachers' thoughts that are tied to particular classroom behaviors. To raise those thoughts to a level high enough to be useful, however, is harder than it at first appears. As Polanyi (1964) has observed:

> The aim of a skillful performance is achieved by the observance of a set of rules which are not known as such to the person following them. For example, the decisive factor by which the swimmer keeps himself afloat is the manner by which he regulates his respiration; he keeps his buoying at an increased level by refraining from emptying his lungs when breathing out and by inflating them more than usual when breathing in: yet this is not generally known to swimmers. A well-known scientist, who in his youth had to support himself by giving swimming lessons, told me how puzzled he was when he tried to discover what made him swim; whatever he tried to do in the water, he always kept afloat. (p. 49)

We selected our cases in several different ways. The first teacher was known to us as an outstanding undergraduate student in education and recommended by her principal during her first year on the job. Our work with her spanned two academic years. Herbert and Keller report the results in Chapter 3. After we were nearly finished with the first case, we began developing the second and third cases during roughly the same time. Both the second and third teachers had about 20 years' teaching experience. We chose one on the basis of the behavioral observations of her classroom; the cluster analysis had revealed that she was a member of an effective subtype. McShane and Cox describe this teacher in Chapter 4. The other, a woman widely recognized for her teaching skill and compassion toward students with learning problems, had served in several leadership positions in her school district and came highly recommended by her principal and by a former colleague who was also a member of our research team. Nowacek and Saunders report on this teacher in Chapter 5.

After developing these three cases we took on two more—one a teacher in a self-contained special education classroom, the other a student teacher. Lindsay and McShane describe the self-contained case in Chapter 6. Manke and Norman report their work on the student teacher in Chapter 7. Our intent in these latter cases was to examine the propositions about effective teaching formed in the earlier cases in some markedly different situations.

Investigators worked in pairs with individual teachers. For each case, they interviewed the teacher with whom they worked to gain some understanding of her personal and professional history and her philosophy about teaching, learning, and the role of children in the classroom (paying special attention to her views of mainstreamed students with disabilities). Next, using the same observation system employed with the clustering procedure, they compared their teacher's in-class behaviors with behavioral profiles established earlier. One team member then videotaped the classroom teacher six to nine times during reading or language arts instruction. The other investigator collected ecological notes on classroom interactions six or more times, occasionally overlapping with videotaped sessions.

After each videotaping, the investigators reviewed the lesson to see whether it was of good audio and visual quality and to determine whether we had captured at least six interactions between the target mainstreamed student and the teacher. If the videotape met these criteria, it was used to conduct a stimulated recall with the classroom teacher.

During a stimulated recall session, the videotape and an audio recorder were played simultaneously. At points of interest (particularly ones where there were nonverbal or verbal interactions between the teacher and the mainstreamed student) an investigator stopped the videotape and asked the teacher to recall what she was thinking about. The investigator also encouraged the teacher to stop the videotape at any time to make comments about activities of interest. All comments were then transcribed and analyzed.

During analyses, team members worked independently to code teachers' behaviors. For the few instances in which there were disagreements, they reviewed videotapes of lessons on which stimulated recalls were based, stopping at those points where videotapes had been stopped for an investigator to ask questions or for the teacher to make comments. Team members then discussed their perceptions of the behavior until they reached consensus.

The investigators then analyzed the content of teachers' thoughts relative to coded behaviors. They allowed the categories of thoughts to emerge from our data. In each case, what evolved from analyses of transcripts was what Erickson (1986) refers to as "units of action"— thoughts and behaviors that are linked. These, in turn, served as the grist for development of themes that cut across the cases. To be considered a theme, thoughts about particular behaviors had to be expressed more than once in a single lesson or be expressed in more than one lesson. Ecological notes served primarily to verify these themes and to identify additional ones when it seemed justified.

In some cases students' reactions to their teachers' behavior were also sought using the same tapes that had been used with the teachers. This allowed us to check the fit between teachers' intent and students' perceptions of this intent.

Our general strategy in the five case studies was to view each case as a replication and extension of the previous case (Yin, 1984). The themes, then, were treated as propositions about effective teaching to be tested in different settings with different teachers. They were scrutinized in classrooms and then brought back to meetings of the case study research teams to be tempered and, in some instances, recast (Lincoln & Guba, 1985). In Chapter 8, Ellwein took a different conceptual pass at the cases by considering the metaphors for teaching implicit in the language, thoughts, and behaviors of the teachers. Her analysis of the five case studies consists of an examination of the case authors' representations of teachers' explanations of their practices. Ellwein did not join the research team until after collection and analysis had occurred, and her participation ended tragically before the completion of the project. Ellwein's distance from the events that gave rise to the cases is both a limitation and a strength. She had to rely on what teachers said and how investigators represented these comments, but she was also free to speculate on these constructed meanings as would any other reader; thus, she demonstrates how to draw meaning from text to inform one's view of teaching.

Ellwein used the cases of Sue and Joyce (Chapters 4 and 5) to explore how their own metaphors of "teacher as author" and "teacher as survivor and manager" informed their actions. She then considered the cases of Marcia, Anne, and Courtney (Chapters 3, 6, and 7, respectively) and suggested other metaphors for teaching practice that arise from their situations. Ellwein's intent was to demonstrate how we can use metaphors that pervade teachers' lives to learn about what it means to be a teacher as well as to stimulate creative reformulations of the job of teacher.

Gallagher, Tankersley, and Herbert (Chapter 9) took into account students' perspectives on teaching and speculated about the nature of communication in classrooms populated by both mainstreamed learning-disabled and typical students. Not surprisingly, they began their work with the belief that students with learning disabilities might have problems understanding teachers' intentions. They thought such difficulties could lead to a downward spiral in communication with teachers and students reinforcing each others' negative expectations.

They built their representation of students' perceptions of teachers and teaching on data acquired from stimulated recall sessions conducted with both typical students and students with disabilities. These students viewed the same videotapes their teachers had seen earlier. They answered questions about what was going through their minds during the course of instruction and about what they thought their teachers were trying to accomplish.

The investigators' analyses of students' responses to teachers' factual and inferential questions revealed notable differences between students with and without learning disabilities. Students with learning disabilities were less able to articulate or infer teacher intent than were the other students in class.

Knowing even with reasonable certainty how successful teachers think and behave in mainstreamed classrooms is a different problem from helping other teachers work in similar fashion. At the outset of this project, we reasoned that in the final phase of our research we should be concerned with translating the results obtained from classroom studies into a language and a set of supervisory methods that would lend themselves to educating teachers in their own classrooms. As a result we designed a study to train supervisors to help teachers reflect on their own situations in relation to the actions of other teachers.

In Chapter 10, Herbert describes how she used a modified multiple baseline design to investigate effects on teachers of using a clinical or in-class process of observation and feedback. Her strategy was (1) to describe over time the thoughts and behaviors of four teachers as they interacted with students in mainstreamed classrooms, (2) to train supervisors to intervene with these teachers in ways that encouraged them to think about their own teaching in relation to our findings about more and less effective practice, and (3) to evaluate the behaviors of typical students and students with disabilities in these classrooms before and after their teachers received supervisory feedback.

One critical feature of the intervention was its emphasis on trying to "transform" rather than "convert" teachers by assuming they hold beliefs about their teaching that direct their actions (Fenstermacher,

1978). Taking a cue from the earlier case studies, Herbert concentrated not only on helping supervisors affect the behaviors of teachers but on what and how teachers thought about their work as well. Her supervisors were trained to begin their work with teachers from the points of view of teachers themselves; that is, supervisors relied on videotaped instructional episodes to elicit teachers' thoughts underlying their behaviors. Once thoughts were made explicit, teachers could compare their own actions with those of the teachers in the case studies. These clinical interventions were supplemented by a journal-keeping procedure that drew attention to their perceptions of their own successes and those of their students. Although all teachers reported high degrees of satisfaction with the process used by the supervisors, the interventions did not appear to influence teachers' in-class behaviors. Teachers' thoughts about teaching and learning changed during the course of their work with supervisors.

THE SOCIOPOLITICAL CONTEXT OF MAINSTREAMING

Implicit in our work has been the assumption that as educators we must look beyond superficial restructuring of teacher preparation at the college/university level and at the school level if we are to help teachers work effectively with students who need special help. We have believed educators need to develop innovations that will better prepare them to be competent in their own areas of expertise while learning to solve problems and to collaborate in meeting the needs of different types of learners. Relationships between special educators and regular educators within teacher education programs, within school systems, and across both levels can either facilitate or inhibit such actions.

Since the enactment of the Education of the Handicapped Act (EHA) in 1975, the majority of children with disabilities have been mainstreamed for some part of the school day. Even so, the practice of mainstreaming students with disabilities into regular classrooms continues to be debated. Disagreements among policymakers, special education teacher educators and researchers, and those who implement policy indicate that we have failed to reach consensus on how children with special needs might best be served (Kauffman, Gerber, & Semmel, 1988; McKinney & Hocutt, 1988; Reynolds, 1989; Stainback & Stainback, 1985; Trent, 1989; Will, 1986; Zigmond et al., 1995). We do not, however, lament the lack of unanimity regarding the best educational placement for students with disabilities. Instead, we see it as a good sign that the field has not adopted *the* one best approach.

Rorty (1991) makes the same point, using philosophy as his example:

> Imagine . . . that a few years from now you open your copy of the *New York Times* and read that the philosophers, in convention assembled, have unanimously agreed that values are objective, science rational, truth a matter of correspondence to reality, and so on. Recent breakthroughs in semantics and meta-ethics, the report goes on, have caused the last remaining noncognitivists in ethics to recant. Similar breakthroughs in philosophy of science have led Kuhn formally to abjure his claim that there is no theory-independent way to reconstruct statements about what is "really there." All the new fuzzies have repudiated all their former views. By way of making amends for the intellectual confusion which the philosophical professional has recently caused, the philosophers have adopted a short, crisp set of standards of rationality and morality. Next year the convention is expected to adopt the report of the committee charged with formulating a standard of aesthetic taste. Surely the public reaction to this would not be "Saved!" but rather "Who on earth do these philosophers think they are?" (pp. 43-44)

While people continue to grapple with the controversial topic of how to educate children with disabilities, teacher education programs continue to be divided along the lines of special education and regular education, and school systems continue to function at odds with the intentions of policymakers who created EHA. Teacher education programs for regular and special education teachers remain largely separate (Sapon-Shevin, 1988; Stainback & Stainback, 1987). Little communication exists between special educators and teacher educators, and students from both programs are rarely enrolled together in education courses. In cases where regular education and special education preservice teachers are grouped together for courses, content is generally not reflective of methodologies and practices used in both areas. Furthermore, coursework requirements for preservice teachers in the two areas do not reflect the spirit of EHA wherein regular and special educators, when deemed necessary, would work together to help mainstreamed students find success in regular classrooms.

Tate (1991) noted, for example, that despite policy advocacy, development, and implementation on behalf of children with disabilities, "as late as 1983 only half of the schools, colleges, and departments of education in states with specific special education requirements had introduced new coursework" (p. 9). He surveyed 64 teacher education programs in four states and determined that for regular education majors, only nine programs required a course in special education, three included aspects of special education as a major part of a course, and four programs infused special education content in their courses. Hence, when we consider the intent of the policymakers who developed EHA, it is difficult to believe that teacher education programs do an adequate job of preparing regular education and special education teachers to implement mainstreaming programs.

As we have reflected on the conduct and results of our study, we have come to believe that separateness also tends to characterize the functioning of regular education and special education personnel at all levels—state education agencies, central office administration, building level administration, classroom teachers, and special education teachers. Even though in our study children with disabilities were mainstreamed into regular classrooms, little evidence exists that special and regular education administrators and instructional specialists coordinated their efforts in areas such as curriculum, instruction, program development, and program offerings. Our interviews with teachers substantiated this conclusion.

SUMMARY

We began our study of what it means to be an effective teacher of mainstreamed students with learning disabilities by relying primarily on research, our own and others, based on behavioral observation of classrooms. We then studied a few teachers in-depth to try to understand why they behaved as they did. In doing so we linked teachers' thoughts and behaviors to form what we called "actions." We refined our conception of the actions of effective teachers over the course of our case studies by examining and refining them from one teacher to the next, and in some cases by comparing them to students' perceptions. We used these actions in our training of supervisors. Supervisors, in turn, intervened with other teachers to encourage them to reflect on their own work. As these events occurred, we gradually became aware of the social and policy dimensions of life in schools in relation to mainstreaming students with mild disabilities into regular classrooms.

NOTE

1. According to the U.S. Bureau of Labor Statistics, 1997, more than half of teachers are women. For this reason, the feminine pronoun is used in this manuscript to refer to teachers though it is recognized that men also teach.

CHAPTER 2

Deriving Professional Knowledge from Cases

Stephen C. Bronack
Lehigh University

Robert F. McNergney
University of Virginia

People learn most from the external world by interacting with it. What our senses take from our environment, our minds interpret, store, recall, and in turn, apply in our future contacts with people, objects, ideas, and events. When the processes of taking meaning from and attributing meaning to the world around us are brought to bear on life in schools, they can strengthen our capacity as teachers to perform to the fullest of our abilities.

We use this chapter to lay the groundwork for "interacting with" the cases in Chapters 3 to 7; that is, to help teachers learn from the stories of more and less successful attempts to work in general education settings with children who have disabilities. The notion of how teachers use knowledge to advance their own professional expertise is central to this task.

CASES AND TEACHING DECISIONS

As a general rule, classroom teachers make roughly one teaching decision for every minute of instruction (Hunt, 1971; Jackson, 1968). The nature of classroom interactions in which teachers are constantly engaged commands rapid, contextually-relevant decision making. Each decision requires the teacher to be keenly aware of the situation in which she finds herself, and to exercise the skills of analysis that successful teachers possess. The dynamic nature of "thinking like a teacher" means being aware of what is happening in classrooms, taking action based on knowledge, and maintaining perspective so as not to be bound by one's own perceptions. The challenge for teacher educators, then, is to assist developing teachers as they continue to hone their decision-making abilities.

Historically, teacher educators have taught decision-making strategies in two steps (Kennedy, 1990). The first step has involved the development of a codified, theory-laden knowledge base—book learning aimed at helping teachers merely acquire knowledge, not apply it. The second step usually includes the development of decision-making skills for situation-based application of the knowledge acquired in step one. Even instruction in practical decision-making strategies, however, occurs frequently in formalized classes on campus. Such environments are often removed both literally and figuratively from real life in schools. Risko (1991) calls the skills taught in these settings "inert" knowledge; that is, knowledge disconnected from real-life thoughts and actions. If aspiring teachers truly acquire knowledge in either step one or two, they still struggle to recall and apply it in real classrooms.

"The challenge," according to Bruner (1996, pg. 17), "is always to *situate* our knowledge in the living context that poses the 'presenting problem.'" In other words, educators must work to make knowledge they offer applicable to a kind of real life where people encounter and must deal with real problems. Scardamalia and Bereiter (1996) offer the concept of *intentional learning*—learning that results when one is actively engaged in trying "to achieve a cognitive objective" (pg. 250)—as an alternative to the type of task-based outcomes found commonly in formalized settings. Their notion of helping people think for the purpose of achieving a particular result, and similar strategies that try to connect learning to real-life contexts, may be especially well-suited to the preparation of teachers. We believe that the use of case-methods for preparing teachers can closely approximate the real-life environment of rigorous decision-making opportunities that classrooms afford.

A *case* is most often a narrative that is set in a real-world context and presented to prompt analysis and action based on tacit knowledge. Case-methodology has played a prominent role in other professional domains for years (Merseth, 1991). Business schools, law schools, and medical training programs have used cases for years as alternative approaches to direct instruction, seminars, and lectures. Only recently has case-methodology gained prominence in the field of teacher preparation (Merseth, 1996).

A case-study method in preservice teacher preparation can narrow the conceptual distance between "the way education life is supposed to be" and "the way it is" by challenging students to examine what they know about teaching and learning and to apply this knowledge to situations they may encounter in their future classrooms (Sudzina & Kilbane, 1992, pg. 153). According to Shulman (1992), cases "may be far more appropriate media for learning than the abstract and decontextualized lists of propositions or expositions of facts, concepts, and principles" most commonly associated with formalized instruction. Teaching cases provide a chance to make judgments and to suggest actions based on the best knowledge available. Merseth (1996) argues that using teaching cases as opportunities for analysis and contemplation fosters *problem-solving and decision-making skills.* When teachers have opportunities to interact with and reflect on representations of real life as they exist in good cases, they imagine themselves actually being in such situations.

Reflection is a useful form of problem-solving that begins well before a problem is formally defined. Dewey (1933) suggested that possibilities for reflection began with some type of cognitive or attitudinal dissonance experienced when encountering a problem. This feeling of discord is brought forth by real-life situations where recognition of trouble in one's surroundings stimulates action toward bringing about "a situation that is clear, coherent, settled, harmonious" (pp. 100-101). When teachers reflect, they think like professionals (Kleinfeld, 1992); they exercise their powers to reason (Sprinthall & Thies-Sprinthall, 1983).

AN ALGORITHM FOR CASE ANALYSIS

We have organized case-based instruction to encourage teachers to think like professionals, that is, to approach teaching as a composite activity involving competing issues, differing perspectives, and possible courses of action emanating from different sources of knowledge that can result in various consequences (McNergney, Herbert, & Ford, 1993; 1994). We have translated this view into a five-step process for analyzing cases. The steps include (1) perceiving issues, problems, dilemmas, and opportunities; (2) recognizing values and perspectives that drive actions; (3) applying appropriate knowledge; (4) suggesting possible teaching actions; and (5) speculating on the possible consequences of such actions (Herbert & McNergney, 1995; McNergney & Herbert, 1998).

As we explain below, these steps are meant to stimulate and sustain professional reflection on case events. The degree to which teachers learn from and later apply knowledge from cases to their real lives depends in no small measure on the verisimilitude of the story and its importance to teachers and on their attention to the five steps.

Issues

Cases are grounded in core issues and relevant facts. These issues are identifiable and provide the foundation for the interpretation of that particular situation. Issues can take the form of problems, dilemmas, or opportunities. Problems are issues that one can conceivably solve. Dilemmas are unique problems that have no apparent solution and, therefore, require some type of coping mechanism. Opportunities are simply possibilities for improving on situations that appear to be working satisfactorily in their present condition.

A prospective teacher in a case-based course said this about the value of identifying issues in a case:

> While students in other courses were making bulletin boards, we were dealing with real-life situations, ones that we will encounter in the field. This course helped me to realize the many problems that occur in schools and ways to handle those problems.

Perspectives

What people see in a situation depends on where they stand. Stakeholders often perceive different issues and assign varying levels of importance to the issues. In real life, when they fail to decenter—to view a situation from more than one vista—the result can be difficult, contentious, even disastrous. Perspectives, fully and fairly represented, influence which issues dominate discussion and which ones are delayed for the time being or are passed over altogether.

A teacher's perspective on life in classrooms is heavily informed by the beliefs and images she holds about students, teaching, and the essential qualities of learning. Teachers make decisions based largely on the interactions of these beliefs and images. For this reason, an essential component of the case analysis process is an identification of multiple perspectives and values held by stakeholders in the case. In teaching cases, these stakeholders can be students, parents, principals, other teachers, indeed anyone involved in or touched by the story.

Cases provide chances for teachers to consider the many perspectives naturally associated with each situation. When a teacher views a case from a perspective other than her own, the issues identified earlier can vary in importance or disappear completely, only to be replaced by new ones. As instructors of case methods, we do not expect this step to change people's own views but we think that considering different perspectives should at the very least raise doubts in some minds. A good discussion that airs different points of view often creates a healthy disequilibrium in a group's thinking about a case.

We perceive some social-psychological danger in this step; that is, a casual consideration of perspectives can easily result in a kind of cultural relativism—one person's perspective is as good as another's. When we teach using the five steps, we take care to caution students that (1) we must consider multiple perspectives in a case, but that (2) some people in the case may be more credible than others, their views more germane. Exactly which people are worth listening to, and in what ways their perspicacity may reveal itself, are open to question.

Figuratively stepping into another person's shoes allows us to be that person—to identify with his innermost thoughts and emotions, to imagine being in his situation. When the story is rich and the discussion round and full, the perspectives represented in the case, indeed the case itself, can become models or metaphors for our own lives—"I might be this person. I might value what this person values. I might be in this situation. I might have to do something to make matters better." These activities seem important in the development of a teacher as a teacher. And most if not all are absent from the more formal, decontextualized approaches of preparing teachers. As one student in a case-based course commented, "To see how people reacted to the situations in the case gives us a running knowledge of how things could happen and what we could do to change them."

Knowledge

The possession and application of knowledge distinguish teachers as a community of professionals. What we know as a profession emanates from practice, research, and theory. No single source of knowledge is perforce better than another. The knowledge most useful to professionals is that knowledge which is most defensible, and defensibility is most convincing when it is measured in terms of the results of knowledge applied—if it works, it is useful.

Curricular materials, previous experience, ideas of colleagues, theoretical treatises, and the like, all may be valuable resources for guiding one's actions as a teacher. The concept of community is important to the development of knowledge as well. In a professional community, knowledge is shared. Knowledge applied to cases provides opportunities for professional peers to benefit from the knowledge held by one another. Bruner (1997) suggests "There are things known by each individual . . . more still is known by the group or is discoverable by discussion within the group; and much more still is stored somewhere else–in the 'culture'" (pg. 52). For these reasons, good, solid casework done by groups of professionals has much to recommend itself.

Action and Consequences

At some point in a situation, a teacher must take or defer action for the purpose of producing desirable results. Teaching actions are typically aimed at compensating for, remediating, or capitalizing on circumstances. The professional propensity for action makes steps four and five critical junctures in the process of case analysis, for they yield demonstrable indications of how and why teachers think as they do about their work. Teachers' actions and the consequences of these actions offer direction for improving that work.

Most teaching situations are complex. They do not lend themselves to the one-right-answer or the one-best-action approach to teaching. Instead, it is quite possible that many defensible courses of action exist for any given teaching situation. A knowledgeable teacher might decide to address issues embedded in a particular case in several different ways. This view frees a teacher to consider varying courses of action she *might* take instead of looking for the one "correct" answer that might exist in the mind of someone less knowledgeable.

If a teacher's actions work, they are "right" or "correct." Although there are many indicators of teaching success and failure, ultimately the proof of whether a teaching action "works" can be found in the actions and learning of the students. Good teaching yields actively engaged, productive students who are motivated and capable of continuing to learn in the absence of a teacher. As many experienced teachers are well aware, however, despite our best intentions, not all actions result in desirable consequences. We believe the more teachers have opportunities to predict and judge the consequences of their actions in cases, the more likely they will be to perform these professional behaviors successfully in real life.

CONCLUSION

The five-step process of case analysis described above is not a recipe to be followed in linear fashion. Sometimes we encourage students to start at step one by identifying issues and work their way straight through to step five—speculating on likely consequences. But sometimes we suggest that teachers begin by imagining desirable consequences and work their way backward to identify the issues that can most readily be tied to those consequences. At other times we encourage students of teaching to jump into the middle of the analysis process by thinking about what they know, or what more they would want to know if they were in the situation, and work both ways.

In real life the journey from one end of the process to the other is rarely a direct one. In our own teaching of cases we try to reflect the interactivity, the interdependence of the steps, but do so in a way that allows us to attend to all five. We may go deeper into the knowledge phase with one group at one time and concentrate more on consequences or perspectives with another group. But over the long term we try to communicate, both verbally and through our choice of activities, a sense of the importance of thinking carefully through all five steps.

In Chapter 8, Ellwein suggests that instructors can teach cases as *representations* of classroom life which portray wisdom and insight about teaching garnered from experience and previous understandings. Case-methodology offers one means through which students of teaching can learn to "play the game" of teaching within the relatively safe confines of a case discussion. And if they play well, they can craft images of the teaching profession that might usefully guide their behavior later in classrooms.

In the end, the images we hold about teaching greatly influence the evolution of our professional knowledge. As we interact with the cases that follow in later chapters, we find ourselves re-examining the judgments, biases, goals, and actions we consider good and appropriate for successful classroom life. Occasionally, what we "know" about teaching is challenged, and we must accommodate both our knowledge and our images accordingly. The cases suggest to us that there is more to professional knowledge than the formulation of principles and axioms which correspond to desired outcomes. The term "professional knowledge" connotes a community of individuals—in this case, teachers and other educators—engaged in action and inquiry specifically designed to help students learn. Teachers who bring professional knowledge to bear address real-life problems in a recursive manner, one that produces action congruent with the mores of the larger community of teachers and educators.

Deriving such professional knowledge is not a matter of gathering as many "tricks of the trade" as possible. Instead, it can be described better as the practice of becoming increasingly cognizant of the factors that most concern the majority of stakeholders. Such awareness is constantly in development and is best achieved when one is immersed in situations that require recognition of these factors in the process of solving *real educational problems*. The residue of acting in such situations is not simply an additional tool or two to use in another similar situation. Learning from cases can be measured in terms of understanding what it means to act professionally. Perhaps the ultimate goal of studying cases of teaching and learning is not always to know *more*, but rather to know *better*. We trust the following cases will prompt readers to reconsider their images of teaching, teachers, and students and to understand better the knowledge that emerges when they interact with the cases.

CHAPTER 3

Marcia Sampson: "If You're Not Teaching, the Students Are Not Learning"

Joanne M. Herbert
University of Virginia

Clayton E. Keller
University of Minnesota Duluth

Marcia Sampson, a beginning teacher in an inner-city elementary classroom, is the subject of this case study. We observed Ms. Sampson during the second semester of her first year of teaching and during the first semester of her second year. She was selected for in-depth study because of her outstanding reputation both as an undergraduate education student and as a beginning teacher.

THE COMMUNITY AND THE SCHOOL

Charter Hills, where Marcia Sampson teaches, is a cosmopolitan community located in a state on the eastern seaboard of the United States. With its temperate climate, natural beauty, historical landmarks (one of which is a large university), and proximity to metropolitan areas, the city has attracted a diverse population of approximately 40,000 embedded within a metropolitan area of about 100,000.

Public schools are located near residential areas and include six elementary schools (grades kindergarten through 4), two upper elementary schools (one for grades 5 and 6, the other for grades 7 and 8), and one high school, as well as a technical education center shared with the county. Of the approximately 4,500 students in grades kindergarten through 12 at the time of this case study, 58 percent were Caucasian, 39 percent were African-American, 1 percent were Asian-American, and 2 percent were of other ethnic descent. Due in part to the community's stable economy, per pupil expenditures and teachers' salaries were higher and pupil-teacher ratios were lower than those for neighboring counties. The school system also ranked first in the state in the percentage of fully certified teachers and first in the percentage of teachers who held advanced degrees.

Ms. Sampson's school, Meade Elementary School, is located in one of the oldest residential areas of the city. This area was once resplendent with large single-family dwellings, many of which fell into disrepair when converted into rental units during the late 1960s. The school, built in 1932, was the first elementary school in the city to be renovated.

During the case study, 455 students attended the school. Forty-nine percent of these students were minorities (three-fourths of whom lived in a nearby housing project), 65 to 68 percent were from single-parent families, and 80 percent were on free meals. According to the principal, the majority of students were deficient in language skills; for the past few years, they had been the lowest-scoring elementary group in the city on standardized tests. Because of the needs of the students, Meade School was usually allotted one extra teaching position to allow for lower pupil-teacher ratios.

THE TEACHER

Marcia Sampson remembers the many hours she and her younger sister had spent playing school, saying, "I knew as early as age five or six that I wanted to be a teacher." Though her mother, a former classroom teacher, and her father, a businessman, expressed concern about low teacher salaries, both encouraged and supported Ms. Sampson's decision to become a teacher. Like her, they felt that personal satisfaction was more important than financial gain.

After high school, Ms. Sampson left her home in the northern part of the state to begin a program of study at the university in Charter Hills. Three years later when student teaching assignments were made, Ms. Sampson's placements were at two nearby public schools. Her success in both settings, her easy rapport with staff and students, and the air of friendliness about the entire school system impelled her to accept a job offer from the Charter Hills Public Schools rather than from the much larger and higher-paying public schools in her hometown.

Both Ms. Sampson and her principal describe her year as a beginning teacher in a fourth-grade classroom at Meade School as a "real shock." Students at Meade, predominantly from low-income homes, have had a history of poor performance in school—a situation quite different from Ms. Sampson's student teaching experience. She found that she had to interact differently with her new students, imposing more structure than she had imposed in other classroom situations. According to Ms. Sampson, students in her practice teaching placements seemed to have had more direction from home and more rules and, as a result, seemed to know what behaviors were appropriate. As she describes the difference in students, she says, "I didn't feel like I had to be so mean, or so tough [with students last year] because I felt like we understood each other. . . . [Here] you have to be mean and nasty for them to understand that you're mad, to a much further extent than I would ever want."

According to her principal, when faced with a challenging situation, Ms. Sampson does not take the easy way out by blaming parents or the school system for students' lack of skills or lack of discipline, but rather tackles students' problems with "missionary zeal." Her boyfriend is overseas, and Ms. Sampson makes school the focus of her life, spending many hours beyond contract time planning a program for her students. In addition, to make ends meet, Ms. Sampson works three or four nights a week as a waitress in a local pub. Despite her busy schedule, Ms. Sampson seldom overlooks an opportunity to improve her teaching skills.

At the end of her first year of teaching, Ms. Sampson had a difficult decision to make: She could either return to the middle school where she had done her student teaching or remain at Meade. She decided to remain at Meade, volunteering not only to instruct a class of 16 "high-risk" students, but also to write during the summer a language arts curriculum that might be suitable to the needs of her future students. She intended to use many of the same teaching strategies she had used the year before, methods she had learned in undergraduate courses and from the reading of Good and Brophy's *Looking in Classrooms* (1994).

The curricular plan she designed for language arts called for whole-group instruction and only minimal amounts of independent seatwork, a strategy the principal also favors. She feels that high-risk students in particular are often ignored by their teachers and given seatwork that is difficult and frustrating. Ms. Sampson believes that the best way to maximize learning time is by teaching or monitoring students throughout the day. This type of teaching behavior is very different from what she has observed in others' classrooms:

> It makes me angry to go by teachers' rooms and see the kids doing independent work first thing in the morning—that's the very time [students] are freshest. Also, some of the teachers often sit behind their desks while students are working. If you're not teaching, the students are not learning.

In addition to her emphasis on active teaching, Ms. Sampson's plan included four components: oral language, reading and literature, written expression, and grammar and spelling. The main focus, however, was to be on reading and literature. Rather than use the basal text, a series that had been boring for her unsuccessful readers, she elected to use a program containing high-interest, low-level stories. She also planned for her students to read several novels, to spend 10 minutes per day reading materials of their choice, to read aloud to her at least once a day, to listen to stories and poems which she would read aloud to the class, and to write daily in their journals.

Ms. Sampson enjoys the flexibility she was given to design her program. It gives her a feeling of control—not a dominating, pernicious sort of control but the sense of being a leader in charge of something important, a feeling she suspects other workers seldom experience. No one is looking over her shoulder, supervising her every move. Instead, she is offered support and is allowed flexibility in her classroom to "think constantly about the minds of sixteen students and the activities in which they were involved."

Describing herself as "self-critical," Ms. Sampson works constantly to find better ways to help her students learn. Her energy seems boundless. If she feels herself relaxing at her desk for too long, she chides herself under her breath, saying, "Come on, Marcia, you're not out there teaching. And if you are not teaching, the kids are not learning."

THE STUDENTS

Many of the students in her first year of teaching had repeated at least one or more grades. Ms. Sampson believes they are easily distracted and need considerable guidance. During her second year, she finds students even more challenging because they are "unmotivated by traditional teaching techniques" and uninterested in schoolwork. Many of the second-year group read at least two years below grade level, score below the 10th percentile on standardized achievement tests, and are considered by the principal as unlikely to complete high school.

During these two academic years, Ms. Sampson works with two boys with learning disabilities: Fred the first year and Tony the second. Fred is a slightly built Caucasian boy who looks young for his nine years. He spends about 45 minutes of each school day in Ms. Sampson's classroom for language arts and reading instruction and the remainder of his day in a self-contained special education class. Although Fred seems shy with Ms. Sampson and other students, he often raises his hand to respond to questions Ms. Sampson directs to the class as a whole. More often than not, however, Fred's responses are incorrect. Ms. Sampson seems particularly concerned about how this might affect Fred's self-esteem:

> He needs lots of one-on-one help. . . . He is one who seldom gets the answer correct, so if he is even close to it, I make a big thing of it. . . . I'm sensitive to his responses. I know he doesn't like coming in here with these big kids like Preston. The students in his [special education] class are much younger.

Unlike Fred, Tony, an African-American student, is integrated into Ms. Sampson's classroom for much of the school day, including the reading and language arts classes. Tony also receives services from the school's learning disabilities teacher in a resource room. He is a fairly quiet boy, handsome and muscular.

Tony has a tendency to be inattentive during instruction, slow to start on his work, and unproductive on assignments, choosing to fiddle with materials in his desk rather than deal with the task at hand. Ms. Sampson often checks on him, redirects his attention, and cues him to the correct spot in the book or assignment. Occasionally Tony becomes disruptive or acts silly if he cannot perform an assigned task or if there is a lack of structure. Socially, he is on the fringe in his classroom; his classmates seem to either tolerate him or ignore him. Despite these shortcomings, Ms. Sampson finds many strengths on which to capitalize. One of these is Tony's love of books:

> He's unbelievable at looking at books. You could get him to look at books for days. I've never seen anyone totally fascinated by pictures in books. "What's this? What's this?" And he always wants to share what he reads.

A TYPICAL LESSON IN MS. SAMPSON'S CLASSROOM

As the 8:05 bell sounds, most of Marcia Sampson's students are at their desks eating the doughnut and drinking the milk they had been given as they passed through the auditorium on their way to class. Located just outside Ms. Sampson's classroom, the auditorium is a busy and often noisy place which serves as the distribution center for breakfasts and lunches shipped in from another school, the gathering place for students during school assemblies, and the classroom for the school's vocal music teacher. Eager to shut out the noise, Ms. Sampson quickly moves to the back of the classroom to close the door; but before she can do so, Lamont slips through the doorway, performs an imaginary slam dunk as he passes Shawn's desk, then settles into a desk near the back of the classroom. Tony, seated on the front row, turns around to grin at Lamont, then continues eating his breakfast.

There are 14 students present: 7 boys, (4 African-American and 3 Caucasian), and 7 girls, (5 African-American and 2 Caucasian). Seated at desks arranged in rows of four, the students vary greatly in size and maturity, with the larger students sitting at the back of the classroom. Although these are fourth-graders, one student, Alonzo, looks as if he could be in high school.

Maneuvering her way to the chalkboard at the front of the classroom, Ms. Sampson exchanges greetings with several students, adjusts the position of one student's desk, then announces that students should finish their breakfasts, start cleaning up, and get ready for their reading lesson. As the 14 students amble between their desks, the trash can, and their lockers, Ms. Sampson adds some tape to the back of one of several posters lining the walls of her bright and uncluttered classroom. This poster, a photograph of a professional athlete, bears the inspirational message "Get an A. Make it a Major League Year."

Moving back to the front of the room, Ms. Sampson pauses at Tony's seat long enough to help him get his papers and books organized, then glances around the room. "Nikuyah, please get your reading book out. Josh, ready? Alisha, put that away, please. All right, everyone, focus."

> I want everyone to be calm, situated, and ready to go. I hate it when they're even moving or doing anything when I'm ready to start a lesson, so I don't like to begin unless everyone is totally ready. . . .
> "Focus" is a little magic word that means for them to stop whatever they are doing, to stop talking, to look up. If they are at their regular desk, they need to straighten it and look up.

As Tony hears the word "focus," he closes his notebook and looks up thinking, "Ms. Sampson wants us to sit up straight, be quiet, and listen." He, like the others, turns his attention to his teacher.

Perching herself on a stool at the front of the classroom, Ms. Sampson says, "Let's talk a little about—James, eyes up here—the story we read yesterday." She gets up from the stool, walks across the front of the room, looks around at her students, then asks, "Who remembers the name of the story we read?" Fingering a piece of chalk, she walks back toward the stool, shifting her gaze from one student's face to another. Five students raise their hands to respond. Ms. Sampson continues to look at her students and says, "Remember? 'The Long . . . " Natasha?"

Natasha: "'The Long Cold Sleep.'"

"Yes, 'The Long Cold Sleep.' And what was 'The Long Cold Sleep' about?" Leaning against the chalkboard, Ms. Sampson again pauses, studying the faces of her students.

> This group is so low that wait time is really important. . . . It takes some students a long time to get the answer right. . . . They'll have to sit there and think and think and then they'll raise their hand.

Smiling, Ms. Sampson says, "Charles, can you tell me what the story was about?"

Charles: "It was about animals."

Brushing her hair from her eyes, Ms. Sampson says, "And? What else about the animals?"

Charles: "And the way they go to sleep."

Ms. Sampson nods and says, "Yes, the way they go to sleep. Can someone tell me the word that he is talking about for when they go to sleep . . . a special word for animals going to sleep?" Ignoring a student who calls out an answer, Ms. Sampson pauses, saying, "I see a bunch of hands. Good hands!" Immediately several hands go up.

I want to keep the students with me and get more students involved. By doing this it allows for more wait time—more time to think. [By saying "good hands"] I'm also praising them for taking a chance. That seems to encourage them to try to answer questions. I worked with that technique when I was student teaching.

Satisfied that the group is involved with the individual answers, Ms. Sampson again addresses an individual student.

"Alisha, do you know?"

Alisha: "Hibernate."

"'Hibernate.' Right! When an animal hibernates, what happens inside their body?" As she says "body," Ms. Sampson stretches her arms out in front of herself. After a moment's pause she says, "Remember we talked about a couple of things slowing down? What happens inside the animals' bodies?" Hands in pockets, Ms. Sampson walks to the side of the room, pauses, then calls on Ron.

Ron: "Their heart stops beating."

Tapping her chest slowly, Ms. Sampson says, "Their heart doesn't stop beating, but what happens to it?"

Ron: "Oh, it starts going slower."

"It starts going slower. Right, Ron. Good." Still holding her hand across her chest, Ms. Sampson adds, "It doesn't stop totally, or what would happen?"

Almost in unison, the group responds, "It would die."

"Right, it would die. When animals hibernate, their heart slows waaaay down." Ms. Sampson says this last phrase very slowly while tapping her chest with a slow, steady rhythm. "What else slows down?" Raising her own hand, Ms. Sampson says, "Raise your hand if you can tell me what else slows down." Again there is a pause.

I know I don't want them calling out answers. I want them to raise their hands.

Smiling, she says, "Remember? Chris?"

Chris: "The way they breathe?"

"Their breathing rate slows way down. Right. Instead of breathing," Ms. Sampson demonstrates rapid breathing, "fast like they do during the spring, summer, and fall, their breathing slows waaay down." Ms. Sampson breathes very slowly.

> Sometimes I try to act out whatever it is I'm talking about just to keep their attention because I like to act and I think they respond better to it. So I am just showing them the difference between regular breathing and slowed-down breathing because I am hoping that maybe I'll catch somebody who isn't quite sure what I mean.

Pacing slowly across the room, hands in pockets, a puzzled look on her face, Ms. Sampson continues to ask questions about concepts in the previous day's story. At one point, she calls on Tony, her student who is in special education.

> I want to see how much he knows because, of everyone in here, I think he might have a lower retention rate. . . . I just want to see how much he got from yesterday. I know Erin and the other kids know.

Directing the students' attention to the front board, Ms. Sampson asks students to give her facts about each of the six animals they have studied. As the students respond, she writes their comments on the board.

> I want to outline for them the facts that they have learned. Just helping them remember the main facts. There are also some words—like "nostril"—that I want to put on the board and get them familiar with again, because they're going to be rereading the story and I want them to be able to identify the words themselves. . . . I'm hoping if I put them on the board, that will give them more time to see them before they reread the words.

After the six columns of facts are complete, Ms. Sampson smiles, gestures toward the board, and says, "Look at all the facts you've listed on the board! You know a whole bunch about animals and what they do in the winter!"

I want them to feel proud of how much they know—that they are authorities on animals. Because they do know a lot when you look at it up on the board. I want them to see that they know maybe four facts about six different animals and that's a lot for little kids!

The clock in Ms. Sampson's room now registers 8:35, and although the students have been attentive during this first segment of the lesson, some are beginning to get restless. Quickly she moves to the left side of the front board and points to a list of vocabulary words, saying, "These are some of the words we had in our story yesterday." As she pronounces the words, several students say them with her. "Yesterday when you were reading aloud, I noticed that a couple of people were saying—Steven, put that away, please—I noticed a couple of people—"(Moving forward, she takes a sheet of paper from Tony, "We're not doing this now")—"said some of these words incorrectly, and I want to make sure you can say them right."

> Steven is playing with his eraser. . . . It bothers me when they have anything in their hands and they are playing with it. And then Tony gets out a piece of paper. Anytime he thinks I'm not looking he'll pull out something else.

One hand pointing to the vocabulary words listed on the board, the other hand on her hip, Ms. Sampson continues the lesson, first asking an individual to say the word, then having everyone repeat the word. When Tony and Jon fail to recite the first word with the rest of the class, she says, "I didn't hear Jon and I didn't hear Tony." Both students immediately repeat the word; then Ms. Sampson has the entire class again say the word.

> I call on Tony and Jon on purpose because they both have the hardest time with new vocabulary words. I want them to say that word aloud so that at least when they come across it in the book, they will be able to say it correctly.

On the second vocabulary word, Tony again fails to recite with the class. Looking down at Tony, who is seated right in front of the word list, Miss Sampson says, "I didn't hear you say it." Tony mumbles, and Miss Sampson says, "Can't hear you say it still. 'Protected.' Say it."

Tony responds quietly and Ms. Sampson says, "'Protected.' Everyone say it one more time—Steven, sit up."

> It looks like I'm picking on Tony, but I ask everyone to say the words. . . . Everyone in the class is trying to say the words except him. And he knows I am standing right there and I can see him. I don't want him to think that everyone means everyone but him. That's why I keep telling him, "Tony, that means you, too."

When Ms. Sampson reaches the fifth vocabulary word, she says, "This word is a tricky one." She pauses, smiles as hands begin to go up, then says, "It means the same thing as sleepy. Remember?" At this point every child in the class, including Tony, has a hand in the air to respond. After calling on Tony to pronounce the word, she nods her head, repeating the word as pronounced, then looks at David and says, "Now what was that word, David?"

> I am trying to keep David with me. I don't want him to think that since I called on Tony that means that he's free. No one's off the hook!

Once the students have gone through the pronunciation of the seven vocabulary words, Ms. Sampson asks students to give her the meanings of each word so she can write the definitions on the board. Alonzo yawns loudly, and Alisha rests her head momentarily on her desk. As Ms. Sampson proceeds to go through the list, students begin calling out answers and have to be reminded twice to raise their hands.

> They're getting excited. They know this material, and they want to call it out and show me that they know it, which is what happens to them all the time. . . . They also know they are coming up to the point where they're going to read, and they're getting restless. They want to get through the list. I want to get through the list, too. I can see that most of them know what the words mean, but I want a couple of them to hear everything again.

Having completed the review, Ms. Sampson faces the class and says, "All right, the next thing we are going to do is hopefully let you earn back some of the break time you lost earlier this morning—four minutes. What you will be doing is getting with a partner and first reading aloud 'The Long Cold Sleep.' After you finish, you and your partner will work together to write sentences for each of the vocabulary words on the front board."

> I'm trying to motivate them to behave well by giving them some of their break back. They like reading aloud and some of them—all of them—really need to read aloud and practice reading in front of an audience. But I still want to motivate them to be quiet and be cooperative so that they can, as a team, get their break back.

Ms. Sampson next explains the procedures for group work and makes team assignments. Ignoring grimaces and moans from several students, she moves quickly among them, helping students arrange their desks into clusters of two or three. After helping Shawna and Chris get settled, Ms. Sampson kneels down, puts her arm around Shawna's shoulders, and talks quietly to Shawna and Chris.

> Shawna craves affection and likes to be touched. Usually I give her a pat on the back or squeeze her like I just did, just to reassure her that even though the work may be tough, that she will do fine. That way I don't have to say it; I can just show it, and then she will usually warm up and try to work with whomever she is with.

As Ms. Sampson stands up, she looks across the room and says, "James, Alisha, Chris, and Cindy have already gotten to work. Good for you!"

> I'm trying to let them know that I see what they are doing and that I'm proud of how they are working on their own. I think that kids like to hear their names in a positive way. I know I do. So I just wanted to let them know that I could see how they were doing.

With the exception of the students in Tony's group, everyone appears absorbed in work. Ms. Sampson circulates quickly among the students, then moves toward Tony's group. She hands Tony a ruler, slides his desk toward the others, then kneels down to listen to the students read.

> I can see that Tony has completely pulled away from the group, so I am checking to be sure everyone else has started, then go over to help

his group start working together. I hand Tony a marker for his book to help him keep his place. I think the marker might help him think that reading a page is not such a monumental task—that he can do it line by line.

For the next ten minutes of the reading period, Ms. Sampson circulates among the students, checking progress, answering questions, and offering words of praise and encouragement. The room is fairly noisy, but the students are not at all out of control. As she leans down to talk with Chris and Pam, Ms. Sampson glances up at the clock.

I am trying to figure out how much longer the lesson should go. Chris and Pam have already finished, so I'm letting them start on their spelling homework. I've got to check with the other groups, too, because I don't want to have everyone finish except one group. I sort of like to time it, too, because I know others are soon going to get their spelling books out, and then it will be hard to pull everyone back together to go over these vocabulary words.

After moving quickly among the groups, telling them to wrap things up, Ms. Sampson strides purposefully to the front of the room, then says, "Focus." There are sounds of chairs and feet scraping the floor as the students turn toward their teacher.

I am getting ready to give them some closure, and I want everyone's eyes on me so we can review what they have learned. I want to reiterate those vocabulary words—just reinforce those words in their minds again. And I want to know what part of the lesson they have missed—what part I need to strengthen.

During this review Ms. Sampson has the teams of students read their sentences aloud. As she concludes the lesson, she smiles and says, "Good job. You really worked well together."

QUESTIONS FOR REFLECTION

- How would you characterize Marcia's teaching? What models of instruction or teaching approaches does she emphasize?

- Why do you think Marcia chooses these approaches over other methods? Are some of her choices ones you might also make if you were teaching in her context? Why or why not? What might you do differently if you were the teacher of these students?

- Do you think Marcia's choices of teaching methods are effective for the special education students who are integrated into her classroom? Are the reasons for her choices also appropriate for her responsibility of meeting the needs of students without disabilities in her classroom?

- What values drive Marcia's approach to integrating special education students in her instruction? Find illustrations from her lesson to support your points. How do your values about the integration of students with disabilities in general education classrooms compare to Marcia's?

THEMES THAT SHAPE MARCIA'S TEACHING

When we analyzed our observations of Marcia Sampson's teaching and our interviews with her, we identified a number of themes, or patterns of thinking and behaving, that recurred during her interactions with students. We describe these ten themes and, in some instances, illustrate them with examples of Marcia's and her students' thoughts about events or her actions (noted as "Event" in the descriptions that follow). This juxtaposition of teacher and student comments is one way of determining whether or not students understand their teacher's intent. Both Fred, a mainstreamed student with learning disabilities, and Tyrone, a typical student, seem to understand the meaning of Ms. Sampson's actions, though to varying degrees. Fred is less accurate than Tyrone with his interpretations, but it is important to note that he was in Ms. Sampson's classroom only one hour each day.

Concern for Her Students' Self-Concepts

Because Marcia believes that most high-risk students have nearly given up hope of succeeding, she makes a conscious effort to spend much of her time praising students for their efforts. It is important that students feel good about themselves: "I want them to think they are smart. I want them to think that they can do it, because that's half of it . . . If you say, 'I can't do all this,' you won't."

Event: As Ms. Sampson reviews the topic and main idea sentences in a paragraph, she mentions Fred's earlier response, saying he was "almost close to the answer."

Thoughts:

Ms. Sampson: Fred is one who seldom gets the answer correct, so if he's even close to it I make a big thing of it. I tell him that he is close. . . . I think the others think he is not as smart as they are so I am trying to let him know that he is close.

Tyrone: He has to find one word out of the paragraph that explains the whole thing. And she gives him a compliment because he tries.

Fred: [She said] it's almost close to it.

Analysis: Ms. Sampson worries about Fred's self-esteem because of his tendency to give wrong answers. She wants to recognize him publicly to support him in the eyes of the other students, so she mentions Fred's earlier response, even though he does not give the correct answer. Tyrone sees the teacher's recognition of Fred for his effort. Fred thinks the teacher mentions his response because "he is close." Whether or not he understands that his effort in this situation is praiseworthy is open to question. But both seem to perceive her intent.

Awareness of Her Students' Abilities and Needs

Ms. Sampson frequently makes decisions based on her prior knowledge of her students' ability to grasp concepts. She seems to know, for example, which students to call on when everyone is confused and she needs the correct answer to a question. Ms. Sampson also knows which students are most easily frustrated and constantly pulls them into the lesson, checking their understanding and giving them opportunities for success.

Desire for Student Involvement

Ms. Sampson urges students to raise their hands, calls on students even if their hands are not raised, and praises responses. Sometimes she tries to increase involvement by telling students that the material is manageable or easy. At other times, she tries to challenge and motivate students by telling them that a particular question is difficult, just to "wake them up and make them want to be the smart person to answer."

The Importance of Control

Ms. Sampson believes it is essential for the students to think she has control and authority. This concern is demonstrated, for example, when Ms. Sampson insists that students participate in activities. In her mind, letting students off the hook might signal to others that participation is optional. Another way she maintains control is through the use of the word "focus." Both Tyrone and Fred understand the use of this ritual:

Event: Ms. Sampson says, "Focus."

Thoughts :

Ms. Sampson: That's a little magic word that means sit up straight, shut your mouth, focus.

Tyrone: When she say "focus," she want us to sit up straight, be quiet, and listen.

Fred: Everybody got to be quiet and straight up so they would listen and tell her what they learned.

Analysis: Ms. Sampson wants students involved in the lessons, but not to the point that they might "lose it." She wants to make school fun, varying methods of instruction and allowing for more self-expression, but finds that veering from routine procedures is often counterproductive.

Concern about Her Image

Ms. Sampson thinks that it is important to be consistent, particularly with low-achieving students. During her second year of teaching she describes herself as "tougher" than the year before, imposing more rules, steps, and procedures. But it concerns her that others might perceive her as "the Wicked Witch of the West."

Determined and Persistent in Her Efforts to Help Students Learn

During her lessons, Ms. Sampson checks for understanding of words and concepts, corrects misunderstandings, and monitors learner activities. She also reviews and summarizes frequently, sometimes frustrated by her students' apparent lack of understanding, yet determined to "get through" to her students.

Event: Before changing to a new activity, Ms. Sampson reviews the purpose for learning about the main idea.

Thoughts:

Ms. Sampson: You just listen to yourself say it over and over. I feel like the way I explain it . . . I say it so many times, how can they not be following? And yet it seems like they don't hear it. I look out and see all these blank faces, and I figure, well, I better explain this another time and say this another way. I don't feel like they have it.

Tyrone: She want us to learn and go on to higher levels.

Fred: The test is coming. When the test comes, the main idea is going to be in there.

Analysis: Tyrone understands that Ms. Sampson wants them to learn and to stretch themselves to move on to "higher levels." Fred reads her intent to be that of preparing her students to do well on the upcoming tests. Getting things right is important in Fred's mind. Recently, Ms. Sampson has been emphasizing the importance of trying to do one's best on upcoming Science Research Associates (SRA) tests.

Desire to Make Things Concrete or Real

Ms. Sampson wants students not only to hear but also to visualize what she is talking about. She draws pictures, acts out vocabulary words, has students act out words, and uses or has students use vocabulary words in sentences. Frequently she attempts to create relevance by appealing to the students' experiences.

Event: As students are reading a passage about crocodiles, Ms. Sampson asks if students have seen the movie *Jewel of the Nile*. Then she quickly says, "Back to the real world!"

Thoughts:

Ms. Sampson: I am trying to remember when I have seen a crocodile—make it real. . . . I mention the movie, which has a great big crocodile.

Tyrone: [She mentions that movie because] she want to ask us and see—Ask us do we see a real crocodile.

Fred: [She is talking about the movie] because it was the main idea.

Analysis: Through reference to a movie that has a crocodile in it, Ms. Sampson tries to make a connection between the idea of crocodiles expressed in the paragraph and the students' conceptions of crocodiles. Tyrone thinks the teacher mentions the movie to determine whether the students have seen a "real" crocodile, with "real" defined as the one in the movie. It is unclear whether Fred perceives the connection between the main idea of the paragraph and the movie.

Sources of Teaching Methods

Ms. Sampson frequently mentions the origin of various teaching techniques, many of which she has learned during student teaching and in undergraduate courses.

Event: Ms. Sampson calls on Barbara for the main idea of a paragraph, then asks how many agree with Barbara's answer.

Thoughts:

Ms. Sampson: That is a technique from the ed. school: checking to see how many are with you while you remain neutral. Because if I tell Barbara that she is right, I never know how many people do know the answer. So I am trying to ask the question in a way so they won't know if I

	agree or disagree with Barbara. I want them to think on their own.
Tyrone:	She wants to find out do we know the answer. And she—That's why she says do we agree with Barbara . . . She tries to trick us . . . to see, like not showing expressions on her face, to trick us to see are we really ready for topics or not.
Fred:	(No thought)
Analysis:	Ms. Sampson refers to her undergraduate training as the source of a questioning technique she uses. She is trying to keep from publicly sanctioning Barbara's response so as to keep the discussion going, that is, to encourage other students to think about the problem before them without prematurely settling on a response.

Values Teamwork, Concept of Family

Ms. Sampson's thoughts and behaviors indicate that she is trying to "promote teamwork attitudes." For example, after pairs of students complete a writing assignment, she instructs them to put both names at the top of their paper.

Thought:

Ms. Sampson:	I want them to feel like it is both people's work and it isn't just whoever writes it down or whoever has the pencil that should get credit. Both students put thought into it, and both should get credit for the work.
Analysis:	Ms. Sampson also describes herself as having a close relationship with students, almost a "maternal attachment." Ms. Sampson and her students are, as she describes it, "a family."

Frustrated by Time Limitations

The adage, "So little time, so much to do," certainly seems to fit Ms. Sampson. She seems always to be working with a psychological pebble in her shoe, harried and anxious to accomplish things. She is driven to get the content across to the students, saying frequently, "I wish I had another forty-five minutes to work on this topic."

CONCLUSION

According to Ms. Sampson, some of her students—like Tony, the mainstreamed student we observed during our second year in her classroom—have been allowed by other teachers to "just sit and do nothing." Anxious to break this pattern of behavior, Ms. Sampson seems to work constantly to motivate her students. She is in practice a "pusher," never quite satisfied with herself or with what her students are doing. Closely monitoring their performances, trying different methods of behavior management, prodding students to participate, and using various tactics to make the content meaningful, Ms. Sampson is unwavering in her determination to help students learn.

Coupled with this tenacity is a genuine and warm concern for students' emotional needs. In fact, making students feel good about themselves is Ms. Sampson's "number one goal." She praises students' efforts, applauds their successes, and appears to enjoy her time with them:

> This is the best job I could have, despite the low salary. I could never sit behind a desk like you do at other jobs. Here I get to work with children, which is fun. It's hard to be in a bad mood when you are with them. Also, my day goes quickly and I'm never bored.

QUESTIONS FOR REFLECTION

- Which of the themes that describe Marcia's teaching are ones that you would like people to use to describe your instruction? Why are they meaningful to you?

- Which of the themes do you think are the most important for facilitating the successful inclusion of students with disabilities into general education classrooms?

- How do they help meet the needs of special education students in such settings?

CHAPTER 4

Sue Rogers: "We Share Responsibility and Respect Each Other"

Edward A. McShane
University of Virginia

Cynthia L. Cox

This is a case study of Sue Rogers, a teacher in a rural school near the city of Charter Hills. Ms. Rogers was nominated to us by her principal as a teacher who is effective with learning disabled students who are integrated into her general education classroom. She celebrated her twentieth year of teaching at Redwood Elementary School during the year we observed her. While the demographics of Ms. Rogers's classroom have changed over the years, her zeal for "giving these kids something" reflects the intensity and commitment she has brought to her teaching.

THE COMMUNITY AND THE SCHOOL

Along the main highway leading south from Charter Hills lies a mixture of woodlands and farms among gently rolling hills. This is not a picturesque, postcard countryside of affluent horse farms and white rail fences; these farms are small, and the houses, trailers, and country stores along the road belong to working-class people.

Redwood Elementary School, where Sue Rogers teaches, had about 180 students when she began teaching there and remained at that size for the next several years. When we observed Ms. Rogers, there were 328 students, with a projected enrollment of 431 for two years later. The city of Charter Hills is spreading rapidly, and many new homes have been built in the Redwood Elementary School district. A redrawing of district lines also contributed to the school's growth. Redwood Elementary School has occupied the same site since 1905, but it now consists of a 1970s building and a major addition built in the 1980s. Still, the school is overcrowded, and some services are provided in trailers located next to the school.

The students at Redwood Elementary School are from varied backgrounds. Many of them live in comfortable suburban homes, while others are part of traditional rural communities. At the time of the case study, one-third of the students received free lunch. Three-fourths of the students lived with both parents. About half the parents graduated from high school; an additional 30 percent had a college education, while 5 percent held advanced degrees. Seventy-nine percent of the students were Caucasian, 13 percent were African-American, and 8 percent were members of other minority groups. SRA achievement test scores indicated a wide range of reading and math achievement among the students.

THE TEACHER

Ms. Rogers grew up in a small town in Ohio and attended the public schools there. She was the second of six children, and much of her time and energy were used in caring for her younger siblings. Her father, an engineer, and her mother, an interior decorator, encouraged her to pursue many interests, including drama, band, cheerleading, and riding. Although Ms. Rogers is proud to say that she was one of only two females in her high school class to attend college, her highest priority was "to become a good wife and mother." Ms. Rogers says she became a teacher because it was one of few professions open to women, because it was compatible with her ambition to raise a family, and because it would allow her to satisfy her "desire to serve."

Although she planned to teach physical education, Ms. Rogers accepted a job teaching fifth grade and continued to do so for three years until she married. Then she and her husband moved to New Mexico, where their first child was born. Although she occasionally substituted in local schools, she focused for several years on being a homemaker and raising her three children. After several moves, Ms.

Rogers and her husband settled in Charter Hills. With her youngest child entering third grade, Ms. Rogers returned to full-time teaching. She chose Redwood Elementary School, feeling she had something to offer the "deprived" children in this rural part of the county.

Over the years she has maintained contact with the school of education at the nearby university, taking a number of graduate courses and involving herself in various projects. This continuing involvement with the university has allowed her to keep aware of current trends and developments in education, and she has taken full advantage of university resources, for example, referring several of her students for assessment and services at the university's reading center. Other projects with which Ms. Rogers has been connected include workshops on discipline and a long-term involvement with the Direct Instructional System for Teaching Arithmetic and Reading (DISTAR) program. She speaks highly of her training as a DISTAR teacher and confidently of her ability to use direct instruction and other methods from special education. Although elements of behavior modification and direct instruction techniques are still a part of Ms. Rogers's teaching repertoire, her teaching has shifted toward a less-structured workshop approach in reading and writing. She traces her current involvement with teaching writing to her experience in a writing project two summers ago. She participated in the workshop in order to become more effective with her students.

As a result, writing and the workshop atmosphere have become an integral part of her classroom style. She now thinks of herself as a writer and incorporates "writerness" in almost every facet of her life as a teacher. Ms. Rogers reached a turning point in her discovery of writing as a teaching technique when she realized that, even though the writing project gave her "all those beautiful prewriting activities," it also told her to go ahead and write whatever she wanted to write about. Freedom to write as one wishes is central to her use of the workshop approach and determines a large part of her class routine.

Ms. Rogers combines the reading-writing workshop atmosphere with her desire to make her students "good students." When asked what she hopes the children will carry away with them from her classroom, she responds, "To have a love of learning; I want them to just be excited about learning."

THE STUDENTS

Ms. Rogers's class is diverse in its makeup, reflecting an area that is both rural and on the fringe of a big university town. Her students are children from professional families and from families receiving some public assistance. The class contains 30 students, evenly divided between boys and girls, but with only one African-American student.

Ms. Rogers prides herself on being able to give the students a good deal of freedom while still maintaining control. The noise and activity levels are always pretty high but rarely rise to an unacceptable level. She can bring them back down with a word or two. The students work well on their own, often in groups or scattered about on the floor or wherever they chose.

Robby, who is classified as learning disabled and who is integrated into this general education setting, fits in well with the rest of Ms. Rogers's class. He has a circle of friends with whom he always sits during group activities, although he interacts with most of the other students on occasion. He seems socially adept. For example, he often returns from the gym in the middle of a little cluster of boys, all talking about the game they have just played. He is a little taller than most of the others, since he has been held back a year and is a year older. Nice-looking, with brown hair, he is one of the more casually dressed members of the class, usually wearing blue jeans and a t-shirt (as do several other students). He appears to come from the lower end of the fairly broad socioeconomic spectrum in the class.

Robby is one of two children in the class who are not reading at grade level, and he goes out for special education resource help every morning. Still, he has a streetwise sense about him. Sometimes he will direct remarks to the others, such as "No, we already did that one" or "He did so have his hand up first." These comments are not said in a hostile way but seem to be his way of asserting his position as a noticer, one aware of what is going on, even if he is not at the same level academically as most of his peers.

A TYPICAL LESSON IN MS. ROGERS'S CLASSROOM

A morning language lesson in Sue Rogers's third-grade class begins just after nine o'clock as her class starts to trickle back in from the gym. Josh, taking the lead as usual, leads a pack of red-faced boys who all talk at once about who scored the most goals and which team won. A second group of boys pops into the room, including Robby, who is chattering with his two buddies, Jason and Joey. Ms. Rogers greets the children cordially, addressing comments to two or three of them, as the rest of the class filter in. While the students are milling around, taking off sweatshirts, tying shoes, finding books, and trying to get organized, Ms. Rogers gets set up for the first lesson. She gives them a lot of room to get organized by themselves. At 9:05 she gives them the call to gather around her at the blackboard. Her tone is warm and friendly, as if she were addressing a group of peers. Although Ms. Rogers is definitely in control in the classroom, there is still a bond, almost a camaraderie, between her and the students.

Ms. Rogers pulls a chair up by the blackboard in the front of the room and waits for her class to settle on the floor around her in a loose semicircle, as they normally do for these large-group lessons. There is a lot of talking and buzzing going on, but it is not excessive, and Ms. Rogers seems comfortable with it.

To begin the lesson on a writing technique called clustering, Ms. Rogers writes "March" on the board and asks students what the word makes them think of. The students start calling out things like "spring," "St. Patrick's Day," "kites," and "Easter," each contributor explaining personal experiences with activities in March.

> [I'm] connecting what students know with what they're learning and giving them an opportunity [to talk about their personal experiences] as long as it's pertaining to the subject at hand [to] make the linkage between what we know, what we've experienced, and what we're learning in [school]. [I'm] making those connections—you have to.

As Ms. Rogers writes "Easter" on the board, she asks, "Why do I put that in capitals?" Without raising their hands, several students answer, "Because it is a name," and Ms. Rogers repeats that to make a point. Ms. Rogers says to Robby, "Did you have your hand up?" When he answers, "Joey took mine." Ms. Rogers says, "Okay," then she adds, "let's get it going." As she gets more responses, she starts asking how each new word should be connected to words already on the board; it's obvious that she's having them think in "clusters," grouping items by the associations they make.

As the students continue to call out more words, Ms. Rogers offers a great deal of reinforcement. "I heard a good one over here. What was it?" As she gets more associations, she says, "Good, you're starting to put [it] together." She calls on Robin, who pauses for a second, then says that she was only stretching. Ms. Rogers responds, "Oh, you were just stretching. Okay, I thought you wanted to share with us."

> She was thinking enough to want to participate, but what probably did happen was that Terri said what she wanted to say. So I want her to know that I saw her signal and that was just fine. I want her to know that I am interested in what she has to say and I hope that's the signal she gets.

Then, Ms. Rogers listens to a long, rambling response from one of the boys. She offers an occasional "uh-huh" and lets him finish.

> I'm letting Mark discuss this because it's important that he gets out what he wants to say, that the other kids . . . are being polite and listening.

Next Ms. Rogers calls on Donald, who says, "Swimming." When Ms. Rogers asks him where that goes, he says, "March," and several kids challenge him: "It shouldn't go there." Ms. Rogers quiets them by saying, "To each his own; that's how Donald sees it."

> I want them to have this [feeling] "I'm in control; I've got something to say, and I want the world to know it, and what I have to say is important." And I want every one of my kids to have that feeling when they leave me.
>
> I try to give students control of what goes on [because] that is an important thing. I say, "This is our classroom; it's not mine and it's not yours; it's ours." . . . So we share responsibility and we each respect each other.

Most of the children have offered something, and Ms. Rogers brings in the ones who haven't, saying, "Oh, come on, some of you people that haven't been talking!"

> [I said "come on" to the kids] because I want everybody to be involved. The kids know that mentally I keep track of who's been answering. I try to encourage everyone in the class to participate in some way. "Come on, guys" [means] "I know you've got something to say: Now you just think about it yourself."

Ms. Rogers looks over the group and says, "Gretchen, we haven't had you yet." Gretchen says, "Blue skies," and when Ms. Rogers asks where that item goes, the student says, "March," to which Ms. Rogers responds, "Good, we need some here." Ms. Rogers gets some more words from other students, then says, "Cary, I haven't gotten one from you." She then says the same to Mary.

Ms. Rogers waits several seconds for her to respond, then calls on Shauna, who is waving her hand. Shauna says, "Chocolate," and Ms. Rogers asks where it should go. When Shauna says, "Easter, of course," Ms. Rogers asks, "Why, 'of course'?" She allows Shauna to explain her association.

> Students have to learn [how to use strategies] . . . I want them to have that skill. I don't care if they don't learn every little [thing], but if they learn how to get to it [they] can be successful.

Now she goes back to Cary saying, "Here we go, Cary." Ms. Rogers smiles and nods while she waits for Cary to respond. After about 20 seconds, Ms. Rogers helps Cary think of "Easter candy."

> Wait time is so important so that each student can think about [a response]. Waiting seems to encourage them to try to answer questions . . . I was pleased at how many students really were involved and that most of them really seemed to understand.

Several students call out, "Put that with Easter and chocolate." Ms. Rogers says, "Super connection," again reinforcing every association they make.

> Some kids have been taught to fail largely because the learning strategies they were taught did not carry over or were not sufficiently internalized to allow them to handle what was going on further up the line in their education. . . . So I give them lots of practice to be learners and problem solvers.

By 9:15, the room has become pretty noisy; there is a lot of talking back and forth and goofing around. Robby is talking and joking with Matt and some of the other boys. Ms. Rogers quiets them with "Here you go!" in fairly high volume. After they've quieted a little, she says,

"Thank you, Matt; I'd appreciate your paying attention. And doing your own thing."

> I draw the line when they are taking an inordinate amount of my energies. I feel that every child in my classroom is an individual and has individual needs, and sometimes these individual needs can be met in small groups or even large-group activity. But when I am having to spend too much of my planning time and too much of my one-on-one time with one child, or when that child's behavior is preventing the others from learning, that's where I draw the line.

Ms. Rogers calls for more responses and gets about four hands. She praises, "Oooh, look at all those hands."

> I am trying to keep the students with me and get more students involved. By doing this, I'm praising them for taking a chance, and I'm also allowing for more wait time—more time for all the students to really think about it for themselves.

Immediately, more students raise their hands. Ms. Rogers calls on Joey and Darryl, who each contribute. Now Ms. Rogers tells them that they are going to go back to their desks and get out their daybooks to "get down all these wonderful associations." She gives a pep talk about using the associations to write in their daybooks what they feel about March.

> The workshop time provides an opportunity for the children to think and write about their own experiences and relate their writing to a particular content area. This morning writing period is important, because the loose structure allows the students to work on material that relates to other subjects or some of their other projects.

At 9:20, Ms. Rogers says, "All right, go write," and the students bustle around getting settled. There seems to be a lot of freedom to choose where they can work; some of the girls settle together in groups of three or four around their desks. Ms. Rogers circulates around, steering some of the students to get started; then she sits down at the table to begin writing in her own daybook. She scans the room and reinforces, "I really like the way this group has gotten out their daybooks and started to write." It is clear that she likes to have the students think of themselves as writers. Ms. Rogers is convinced she gets better work from her class through this approach, "because the children are now designing what they want to do. It's not what I want them to do; it's what they want to do."

Ms. Rogers tells them, "Maybe around 10:30, we'll sit down and share our thoughts."

> Now my whole morning activities, my whole language arts is a workshop environment. The kids get to choose what they want to read, what they want to write, but they must read and write and . . . share with the group some of what they've written.

There is a little buzzing, and Ms. Rogers says, "Remember how we like to have it quiet? That's how I need it . . . [and you do, too]." She tells them to "just let it flow." She puts on some soft background music and tells them, "Whatever you feel about March, write it down. Keep your pens moving."

The background music is very pretty and mellow, and the room is quieter than at most other times when the children are doing other seatwork. Ms. Rogers has set up a specific environment for this writing time, and the rules seem very well-established. The only sounds are the shuffling of papers, erasing, and shifting in their seats. As the children are writing, some of them stop, look around for a minute, then go back to writing. Ms. Rogers spots Matt fooling around with the stapler on her desk and asks, "Matt, will you please start writing?"

It is now 9:30, and Ms. Rogers is up and moving around again, checking in with individual pupils, and giving feedback. Her presence is unobtrusive; she goes over to one student, Tim, and very gently says, "Your pencil's not moving." They talk back and forth; it seems he's writing something very private and important to him. It is clear from Ms. Rogers's comments that his writing is not exactly about March, the assigned topic, but Ms. Rogers says, "That's okay." They have a lot of leeway in what they can write. Ms. Rogers's tone is very positive and supportive as she talks with Tim. Finally she ends with, "Thanks for sharing," and moves on to Robby with a cheery "All right, Robby my man, how's it going? Do you want to share with me?" As Robby shrugs her off, Ms. Rogers says, "You're not finished; you want to keep on working. Okay."

The room is a little noisier; there is more talking back and forth, and a few students are starting to get up and mill around. At about 9:45

Ms. Rogers says, "Folks, I hear some people saying they want to share right now." When Josh groans and says, "No, not yet," and several others concur, Ms. Rogers leaves it, saying, "Okay, those who want to [share]."

Ms. Rogers says, "I want to see my Unicorns up here," indicating the horseshoe-shaped table in front of the brightly colored rainbow bulletin board containing samples of the students' best writing. While the eight children collect their daybooks and move toward the table, Ms. Rogers points to the board and reviews a list of priorities for students not in the small group.

> I am ensuring everybody knows the priority for what they are to do, because a big thing that we do in the third grade is to teach them how to manage their own time. . . . To [teach personal responsibility] you have to give students time to manage; then you have to be sure that they remember what they have to do. I have the things written on the board, and they can choose their [order] for doing it.

Then Ms. Rogers joins the group of children at the table and tells them, "We are going to do something super today." As Ms. Rogers passes out the papers, she tries to engage them in thinking about how interesting it is whether people take papers off the top or the bottom of a stack. No one responds, and Ms. Rogers moves on with the lesson.

After the children have had a minute to look at the papers, Ms. Rogers checks to see whether they understand what they will be working on today. Several of the students answer in unison, "Questions," as they attempt to read what is on their sheets. Ms. Rogers responds, "That's good you said 'questions,' but that word is 'quotations.'"

> I want the kids with their hands up to respond. I don't expect kids to always know the answers to questions. . . . And I try not to send the message that "If you don't know, that's terrible," but I want to send the message that "Boy, if you do know, that is good."

Ms. Rogers introduces the lesson by telling them that they are "already using and abusing quotations in your writing, and so now you're ready to learn how to use them correctly."

Then I put them into little structured groups and I say, "Okay, now look, you're doing this, and this is what you're trying to communicate and so you need these skills," and that's when I teach them. So now they're using and abusing [quotations], so now I'm teaching it and the kids are sitting there and saying, "Aha," because they've got a hook into what I'm trying to teach as a skill.

Ms. Rogers asks, "What is a quotation?" One girl describes a question mark, and another describes a factual statement. Ms. Rogers says, "Hmmm," and keeps pushing for the answer she wants. She says warmly to one of the girls, "I know you know."

I don't want to tell the students what a [quotation] is. I want them to think and discover [the concept]. They have used quotations in their journals, so I know they know what [quotations] are at some level. So now I want them to give lip service to this discovery that they made.

Robby has been fairly attentive, but he looks down and to the side a lot, especially when Ms. Rogers asks a question. Ms. Rogers says, "Robby, you've used quotations, too, in your writing, remember?" Robby pauses for a second, then says softly, "Yeah." Picking up on the way he said it, Ms. Rogers says, "It's okay if you don't." Ms. Rogers works at keeping Robby involved in what the rest of the class is doing, and she is emphatic about not treating him differently than the other students.

She tells them, "Now we're going to be editors." Sandy reads the first sentence; then Ms. Rogers tells them to put the comma where it belongs. Ms. Rogers scoots over to Terri and walks her through the first sentence. Even though there are eight children sitting at the table, Ms. Rogers monitors what each one is doing, moving quickly from one to another. Ms. Rogers prefers a horseshoe-shaped table because with a kidney-shaped table "you're too far away."

Now Ms. Rogers reviews a punctuation rule by stating a sentence for the students to complete as a group: "The first word has to begin with—okay, everybody?" All the students answer promptly when she gives a hand signal, "A capital!"

I want to review that all sentences begin with capital letters whether they're quotations or are not quotations. This is just a quickie review. . . . I want them to feel really good and substantial about what

they're learning and going to do before they leave me, and [so] prove
to me that they know how to [edit capital letters]. . . . I'm asking them
a total group thing, and I want a response with everybody. It's a quick
way . . . to get everyone's attention and bring them back together, I'm
using this mechanism to do that for a quickie review.

Ms. Rogers continues, "How do you show a capital letter with
editing marks?" Nicole correctly describes the three marks, and Ms.
Rogers asks the other students, "How many students agree with that
answer?" She says, "Right, the three little lines indicate capital letter.
Good being editors!" Now Ms. Rogers goes over how to put the
question mark inside the quotes and has them try it. Ms. Rogers gives a
little pep talk, "Come on . . . Feel comfortable about this . . . I don't
expect you to know this; that's why I'm teaching it." She goes to the
next sentence and has them read it and then put the comma where it
belongs. She looks at Robby and says, "Wow, that was fast," then says
to one of the girls, "I can tell you're feeling better about this already."
Now she says it's time to go back to the beginning and write the
sentences correctly using their editing marks. Shortly after they start
working, Ms. Rogers glances over at Robby, then stops him with
"Whoa, Robby, gotta start over. . . . You didn't start at the beginning of
the sentence." She assists him with the first one, then checks the others,
giving feedback just as she did with Robby.

I asked [Robby] what was said in the sentence because he had not
marked it properly . . . I need him to mark the quotation marks and
then separate who said it from what they said with the comma . . .
Rather than giving him the answer or telling him "no," I'm taking
him back and walking him through it so that he can discover "Hey,
I'm right" or "Uh-oh, I need to do this." . . . And then I check [all the
students' papers] around the table because it's very important to get
the first one done correctly.

While Ms. Rogers works with this group, the rest of the room is
pretty quiet; most of the children are working well on their own. The
group at the table continues to work, with Ms. Rogers watching,
checking, helping them one at a time. At about 10:05, Ms. Rogers tells
them to share their sentences with a partner and check them. After
several minutes of noisy student activity, Ms. Rogers says, "Freeze!"

I'm thinking that the kids are getting a little carried away with sharing their experiences and getting a little restless . . . So I say, "freeze" because it is important they all settle down and listen so I can review, wind things up, and then go over their work priorities for the workshop period.

Once Ms. Rogers has the students' attention, she reviews what they have been working on by asking questions and allowing all students turns in answering.

It is 10:10 when Ms. Rogers starts to wrap up the lesson, telling her students what to do with their papers. As she reviews with them what they have learned, she seems pleased with herself and especially pleased that Robby was involved in the lesson. As the children start to leave the table, she reminds them about their biography assignment and asks what each of them has to do to finish. When Terri responds that she doesn't know how to find out if her person was a patriot, Ms. Rogers asks other students to "tell her what she could do."

She doesn't come up with anything, so [here] are all her peers and now she's going to get all these strategies. She's going to realize these are strategies that the other kids already know and that there are things that she can do. You can see how spontaneous that was! All the other kids in her group just put up their hands to help her.

As the students leave the table, Ms. Rogers announces to the class, "You have about fifteen minutes more to work on your own. Let me know if you're ready to conference." Turning to Robby, she says quietly, "Okay, bye. Tell her [the resource teacher] I'm sorry we went a little over."

QUESTIONS FOR REFLECTION

- How would you characterize Sue's teaching? What models of instruction or teaching approaches does she emphasize?

- What does Sue value as important for her students? Do you think these outcomes are also beneficial for students with learning disabilities? Are there any additional outcomes that you would like to see emphasized?

• What beliefs does Sue hold about the reading and writing workshop approach? Do you share those beliefs? What do you see as the benefits and drawbacks of such an approach with special education students who are integrated into general education classrooms?

THEMES THAT SHAPE SUE'S TEACHING

We identified six themes, or patterns of thinking and behaving, when we analyzed our observations of Sue Rogers's teaching and our interviews with her. We describe the themes, illustrating them with representative classroom events and Sue's thoughts.

Individual Worth

This theme emerges from the statements Ms. Rogers makes about the importance of building strong, positive self-concepts in her students. It includes her active listening, encouraging, and praising.

Event:	Ms. Rogers listens to a long and rambling response from one of the boys. She offers an occasional "Uh-huh" and lets him finish.
Thought:	I'm letting Mark discuss this because it's important that he gets out what he wants to say, and that the other kids . . . are being polite and listening.
Event:	Donald calls out that "swimming" could go with "March," and several students immediately challenge him that it shouldn't go there. Ms. Rogers quiets them by saying, "To each his own; that's how Donald sees it."
Event:	As Ms. Rogers gets more associations from the students, she says, "Good, you're starting to put [it] together."

Active Learning

Ms. Rogers wants the students to take responsibility for their own learning and to be involved in class activities. This theme is comprised of the following: participation and involvement, promoting discovery, internalizing learning strategies, love of learning, and cooperation and teamwork.

Event: Ms. Rogers tries to reassure students by saying, "Come on! Feel comfortable with this. I don't expect you to know all this; that's why I'm teaching it."

Event: On the board at the front of the room is a list of "priority things" that the children know they can be working on whenever they have time. Ms. Rogers had called their attention to today's list earlier.

Thought: I am ensuring that everybody knows the priority for what they are to do, because a big thing that we do in the third grade is to teach them how to manage their own time.

Event: After most of the children have offered something in the initial brainstorming portion of the clustering lesson, Ms. Rogers attempts to bring in the ones who have not contributed by saying, "Oh, come on, some of you people that haven't been talking!"

Thought: [I said "come on" to the kids] because I want everybody to be involved. . . . I try to encourage everyone in the class to participate in some way. "Come on, guys" [means] "I know that you've got something to say. Now you just think about it yourself."

Event :   During part of the lesson, a girl remarks that she does not know how to find out whether her person was a patriot. When Ms. Rogers tries to get her to think of ways she could figure that out, and gets no response, she invites the others in the group to give her some suggestions.

Thought: She doesn't come up with anything, so [here] are all her peers and now. . .she's going to realize these are strategies that the other kids already know and that there are things that she can do.

Event: Ms. Rogers uses a science textbook to teach her students how to use the words in bold print to gather the key information from a chapter. She directs them to look for the vocabulary words which are written in bold print and reviews with them what they can learn without reading the whole page.

Thought: It's really important for them to learn to use strategies. Some kids have been taught to fail largely because the learning strategies they were taught did not carry over or were not sufficiently internalized to allow them to handle what was going on further up the line in their education. Students have to learn [how to use strategies]. . . . I want them to have that skill. I don't care if they don't learn every little [thing], but if they learn how to get to it [they] can be successful.

Teaching Techniques

This theme includes the many effective teaching techniques that Ms. Rogers consciously chooses to use. One of the most salient is the reading-writing workshop approach, which is currently Ms. Rogers's preferred method of teaching.

Event: After writing one or two final responses on the board, Ms. Rogers tells the class that they are going to go back to their desks and get out their daybooks to "get down all these wonderful associations." She gives a pep talk about using these things to write in their daybooks "what they feel about March."

Event: As Ms. Rogers says, "All right, go write," the children bustle around getting settled. Some of the girls settle together in groups of three or four around their desks, and this seems to work out well. Ms. Rogers circulates in the room, steering some of them to get started, and then sits down at the table to begin writing in her own daybook. She scans the room and praises the students: "I really like the way this group has gotten out their daybooks and started to write."

Thought: I get better work from the class through this approach, because the children are now designing what they want to do. It's not what I want them to do; it's what they want to do. Now my whole morning activities, my whole language arts is a workshop environment. The kids get to choose what they want to read, what they want to write,

	but they must read and write and . . . share with the group some of what they've written.
Event:	Ms. Rogers teaches a lesson which integrates the social studies subject matter with the students' own writing. This reflects her belief that the workshop time connects all the various subject areas and provides an opportunity for the children to think and write about their own experiences and relate their writing to a particular content area. This morning writing period, with its loose structure, allows the students to work on material that relates to other subjects or projects.
Event:	Ms. Rogers passes out the papers, and after the children have had a minute to look at them, she checks to see whether they understand what they will be working on in this lesson.
Event:	Several of the students answer in unison, "Questions," as they attempt to read what is on their sheets. Ms. Rogers responds, "That's good you said 'questions,' but that word is 'quotations.'" She introduces the lesson by telling them that they are already "using and abusing" quotations in their writing, and therefore they are now ready to learn how to use them correctly.
Event:	After modeling the task for Jeremy, Ms. Rogers looks over at Robby, who is trying it on his own, and says, "Exactly right . . . but it needs to be before." Her tone with both boys is gentle and supportive. Now she slides over to Tanya and assists her with the first sentence.
Event:	Ms. Rogers models with the group how to do the first sentence. Even though there are eight children sitting at the table, she monitors what each one is doing, moving quickly from one to another.
Thought:	I prefer a horseshoe-shaped table like this because with a kidney-shaped table you're too far away.

Integrating Experiences

Relating new content to what her students already know from their own experiences or to what they have learned from other content areas is the fourth theme.

Event: In a session in which Ms. Rogers combines teaching study skills with a science lesson, she relies heavily on relating the new material to knowledge the children bring with them from their own experiences. She strongly praises their making these connections.

Event: As she has the students look at a picture in their texts and tries to teach them the concept of condensation, one of the girls tells about an experiment they conducted in Girl Scouts. Another girl who had participated in that activity speaks up excitedly and adds a little more information. Ms. Rogers listens, acknowledges that they are on the right track, and then adds, "Wow, and some people don't think the Girl Scouts learn things, and it is both our Girl Scouts who noticed the water on the outside of the glass and said it came from the heat in the air."

Event: After having the class vote on whether they think the ice in another picture in their text is freezing or melting, Ms. Rogers calls on several students to give rationales for their votes. Connie says that the ice looks the same way as when a Popsicle melts, and several others call out, agreeing with her. An impromptu discussion follows, with the students talking back and forth about Popsicles and icicles. Ms. Rogers lets the discussion wind down and then says, "So, we learn a lot from our environment."

Thought: I want to point out what they observe in their environment because I am trying to tie in what they know, their awareness of what they know, and applying it to new information, making the linkage between what we know, what we've experienced, and what we're learning in this book. I give them an opportunity [for free discussion] as long as it's pertaining to the subject at hand.

Awareness of the Special Needs of Her Students

Ms. Rogers has a great deal of information about the special needs of her students, both those special education students who are integrated into her classroom and those who are typical students. She frequently takes this information into consideration when interacting with them.

Event: After the Popsicle discussion, Ms. Rogers continues questioning her students about how they can tell from the picture that the ice is melting. She calls on Robby, the mainstreamed student with learning disabilities, who has had his hand up for several minutes.

Robby says you can tell the ice is melting by "all those little holes with water in them."

Ms. Rogers asks, "Can things look like that when they are freezing?"

Robby answers, "No."

"Only when they're melting," she repeats very emphatically. She adds, "Super observation, Robby, just super."

Thought: Robby needs to know that what he has to say is important, and that was a very astute observation. He has a lot of experience being out in the woods. And I did not call on him when he first put up his hand because I don't want him to always feel that the minute he puts his hand up I'm going to call on him or he'll forget . . . or he isn't like the rest of the kids . . . But he needs to feel like he's part of the group.

Event: Later in this lesson Ms. Rogers has the children read a definition that goes with one of the pictures in their science text. She tells Robby, "If you get stuck, Jody or Jeremy will give you a hand." She repeats these directions to Kathy, who has transferred from another school and is behind the rest of the class in her reading skills.

Event: In a lesson on quotations, Ms. Rogers reminds Robby that he has already used quotations in his writing and asks him, "Remember?" Robby pauses for a second, then looks away, saying, "Yeah," very softly. She responds to the way he says it and replies, "It's okay if you don't."

Thought: [I feel very strongly about keeping Robby] involved in
                  what the rest of the class is doing and not treating him
                  differently than the other kids.

Event: In another lesson, the students are reporting on
                  biographies they have read when Tammy fails to make the
                  connection between the title of her book and the main
                  character. Ms. Rogers provides detailed assistance to help
                  Tammy perceive and express the connection.

Thought: The students in my highest reading groups tend to make
                  these connections on their own, but the children in the
                  "low-level" groups have trouble with that and need to
                  learn how to make these connections before they go on to
                  fourth grade.

Freedom and Control

Ms. Rogers allows a great deal of freedom in her classroom, especially
during the reading and writing workshop times. She draws the line,
however, when she feels she needs to exert control.

Event: As Ms. Rogers says, "All right, go write," the children
                  bustle around getting settled. There seems to be a lot of
                  freedom as to where they can work, how they can cluster
                  together, and what they can write about. Some of the girls
                  settle together in groups of three or four around their
                  desks, and that seems to work well.

Event: The background music is mellow, and the room is quieter
                  than at most other times when the children are doing
                  seatwork. The only sounds are the shuffling of papers,
                  erasing, and the shifting of children in their seats. Most of
                  the children are writing. Some of them stop, look up and
                  around for a minute, then go back to writing.

Event: Mark, who has been out of the room since the writing
                  time started, comes back and fools around with the stapler
                  on Ms. Rogers's desk. It's apparent that he is having
                  trouble getting started. After he has been at the desk for a
                  minute or so, Ms. Rogers, who has been sitting and
                  writing herself, spots him and says, "Mark, will you

please get over here and start writing?" Mark says something about needing the stapler, and she says, "Just do what we're doing . . . quickly."

CONCLUSION

Ms. Rogers's attention to the special needs of her students, her use of strategies to help them become good students, and her belief in the workshop approach as a sort of glue connecting all her language arts teaching are reflected in one final event. At the end of the lesson on quotations, as she reviews with the group what they have done, she is obviously pleased with the lesson, especially with Robby's involvement in responding to all of her questions. Commenting later to us on Robby's participation in that lesson, she says, "That's how you get a kid with a learning disability involved in a lesson, without hanging everything on the area of disability. That's what education is: talking, sharing, communicating." We believe that Ms. Rogers's effectiveness with all her students is based on that statement.

QUESTIONS FOR REFLECTION

- Which of the themes that describe Sue's teaching are ones that you believe characterize your instruction? Why are they important to you?

- Which of the themes do you think are the most important for supporting the successful inclusion of students with disabilities into general education classrooms? How do they help to meet the needs of special education students?

CHAPTER 5

Joyce Wilson: "I Want Their Day with Me to Be the Best That It Can Be"

E. Jane Nowacek
Appalachian State University

Shari L. Saunders
University of Michigan

Joyce Wilson, a fifth-grade teacher in a suburban school near Charter Hills, was selected for our study at the recommendation of her principal. In her class of 24 students, 4 were identified as students with learning disabilities or emotional/behavioral disorders. Ms. Wilson believes that teachers in the lower grades recommend that special education students be integrated into her room because they know she maintains a classroom that meets the needs of these students.

THE COMMUNITY AND THE SCHOOL

Stillwater County, which surrounds Charter Hills, houses a growing middle class who prefer the quiet spaciousness of the country to the noisier city life. Its rolling hills, abundant water supply, and gentle climate nurture prosperous cattle and horse farms. Like Charter Hills, it harbors poor African-Americans and Caucasians whose educational and financial opportunities are as restricted as the boundaries of the hollows in which they live.

Recently this economic and educational diversity has become more apparent in the students enrolled at Jackson Elementary School. The development of housing subdivisions in this once exclusively rural area has increased the school's population about 60 percent in the six years prior to this case. Over half the parents of the 483 students work in skilled occupations and managerial and sales services. Another 20 percent are professionals, and approximately 10 percent work in unskilled occupations. Of the remaining 10 percent, half are self-employed and half are unemployed. Twenty-two percent of the students receive free meals or reduced-price meals. Almost 18 percent of the students live in single-parent homes, and about 19 percent of the school population are members of minority groups.

Rapid growth in population necessitated a physical expansion of Jackson Elementary. During the year of this case study, backhoes and bulldozers arrived to begin work on a new addition which was to include administrative offices, classrooms, a kitchen, and a gymnasium. In spite of the overcrowded conditions and construction noise, the students appear to learn at Jackson. A quiet, efficient atmosphere, reminiscent not of modern factories but of cottage industries, permeates its corridors and classrooms. The school seems warm and caring, yet organized and productive. Students, moving in quiet orderly lines through the hallways, pass beneath colorful paper cutouts of Washington, Jefferson, and Betsy Ross which adorn carefully copied reports. Farther down the corridor a large green sign announces, "Mr. Singleton, the principal, says everyone has a snake story. Here's his. What's yours?" An even larger expanse of yellow paper awaits students' entries.

Midway down this hallway is Ms. Wilson's room. There are no numbers on classroom doors at Jackson. Each door bears the name of the teacher, neatly printed in black Magic Marker. The absence of impersonal numbers fits the family feeling of the school. This fifth-grade classroom exemplifies the quiet and caring efficiency of Jackson School in general and of Ms. Wilson in particular.

THE TEACHER

Joyce Wilson, like the county in which she lives and works, is a product of both economic limitations and growth through higher education. The only one of the 10 children in her family to complete high school, she knew at age 11 that she wanted to go to college, even though she was not exactly sure what college was. She did know that the way to get out of the poverty constricting her life was to get an education.

Although her parents encouraged her educational interests, they were not able to give her financial assistance. She earned money working at a grocery store and the five-and-dime store. With the money she saved from these jobs and with scholarships, loans, and work-study positions, she was able to attend Lincoln College. Ministers and church members continued to help her while she was in college, paying for her linens and buying her textbooks.

Her determination to meet and conquer life's challenges is further exemplified by her choice of college majors. Her selection of religion as one of two majors is not surprising because it had always been influential in her life. However, her choice of English as a second major is revealing. She recalls, "I took some kind of test [upon entering college], and they told me I was a bit weak in English. I wasn't, and I was going to prove them wrong, so I made a joint major of English and religion."

She originally wanted to be a director of religious education and work with adolescents. She took teaching courses solely as a safeguard, something to fall back on. She learned later that being a director required an advanced degree. At that time, married and pregnant with her first child, Ms. Wilson needed a job and could not afford to go to graduate school.

After her daughter was born, she worked as a receptionist for a pediatrician but eventually got a job as a tenth-grade English teacher. This position lasted only three months because she learned she was pregnant with her second child. In 1963, teachers who were obviously pregnant were not allowed to teach in public schools in her state. So in November she was replaced, although her son did not arrive until April. When she chose to begin working again, there were no jobs available teaching English. Consequently, Ms. Wilson took the courses she needed to be certified as an elementary teacher.

Her first elementary teaching position was, as she remembers, in a very "suburban, elite school where all the children's parents were doctors, lawyers, or professional people." She felt she did a good job, but she did not find the work challenging. The children were easy to teach. "It was like opening up their heads and pouring it in, and they gave it back."

Two years later she was transferred to an inner-city school where she taught fourth and fifth grades. She remembers most the diversity of the student population and recalls that moving from a suburban school to an inner-city school was an adjustment.

> I went through cultural shock, and that was when I learned how to teach. . . . I visited every child's home. Regardless of what the situation was or how dangerous the situation was, I went. . . . That gave me an entirely different perspective of how to approach each of those children, and I was able to individualize my approach to them based on what I knew about their background. I think if you don't do that, if you don't get to know the child's home, that you're really missing the boat as a teacher. . . . I thought I was well-planned. Probably my first two or three years of teaching, I may have had a lesson well-planned and may have understood and been able to teach the lesson thoroughly, but I didn't know what to do about these other fringe things that were happening: how to handle eruptions, what do you do when you've got a field trip, and all those things. You just learn how to be a really skillful manager of time and materials and resources.

Ms. Wilson was assigned to another school when district lines were redrawn to effect full integration in the Lincoln schools. Her new students were even more diverse than those in her former school. She describes several of her students as having "emotional problems" and the teaching situation as being difficult. This experience helped her realize that

> there is very little support outside the classroom if you have a child that's going to be a problem. You have got to come up with ways that you can live with that child day in and day out. I run a very structured classroom. It's another part of what I call survival. In order to have a good day and in order for things to run smoothly, you've got to have a plan.

Her determination to survive in the classroom, as well as in life, is tempered with a sense of caring for her special education students.

> If I have these children, it's my responsibility . . . You come up with things that will help you. You find ways to make the child feel good about himself if you possibly can. Sometimes you can't do that. Some children have such a low self-esteem, and it's beyond your power.

The way I approach it is that I want their day with me to be the best that it can be. I want the time that they're here to be happy. I don't want to add to their miseries or add to their problems, so I like to create an atmosphere where we're working together and we care about each other.

A few years later her family moved to Stillwater County. Here Ms. Wilson taught remedial reading to sixth, seventh, and eighth graders and then worked as a half-time sixth-grade reading teacher and half-time administrator for the gifted program. During the next eight years, after earning an M.Ed. in administration and supervision, she held various administrative positions: assistant principal, acting principal, elementary supervisor, and director of instruction.

Because Ms. Wilson believes a good administrator knows what is going on in the classroom, she decided to return to teaching. At Jackson School she once again worked with fourth and fifth grades but for the first time taught students identified as learning-disabled who were integrated into her class.

I really get a kick out of those kids . . . I hope I have rapport with all [of my students], but I think I have a special rapport with the ones that come from a really rough background because I've experienced that in my childhood, and I feel or empathize with what they're going through.

Ms. Wilson's efforts to provide the structure, individualized attention, and security she believes are important to elementary school children are reflected in her thoughts about education:

For me a child has succeeded if he's growing, if he's made progress . . . It's the person that's growing, not the amount of knowledge pouring in because . . . education is learning how to live, and that's what we need to do more with these children. The darn math don't matter a hill of beans if the child doesn't have self-help skills . . . or if he's got emotional problems, or if he's being very aggressive.

This belief is apparent after only a few visits to Ms. Wilson's class.

THE STUDENTS

Ms. Wilson had taught most of the same students the previous year as fourth-graders, so she has had the opportunity to watch them grow and develop over a two-year period. Our focus was not on the class as a whole, but upon one reading group and upon one of its members in particular: Tabatha. These students share similar frustrations when faced with difficult tasks. Of the six children in the group, three boys and one girl, Tabatha, receive special education services, one boy is enrolled in the Chapter One reading program, and a second girl has recently immigrated to the United States. According to Ms. Wilson, the group exhibits a wide range of strengths and weaknesses in the areas of decoding skills, reading comprehension, vocabulary, and writing. In spite of their individual differences, they function as a family and are eager to help one another.

Ms. Wilson told us that Tabatha had been very quiet, shy, and withdrawn the previous year. This year, however, she has "blossomed" and now talks easily with the other students, appearing more self-confident and better able to cope with difficult situations without tears. Tabatha still becomes frustrated with her schoolwork; and although she enjoys reading, she has difficulty comprehending what she reads. She seems to be in constant motion, twisting her hair, shuffling papers, or swinging her legs. This high activity level carries over to her schoolwork, and Tabatha is usually working on a written lesson—whether or not it is the current class activity.

A TYPICAL LESSON IN MS. WILSON'S CLASSROOM

The clock on the back wall of the classroom reads 9:18 as the learning disabilities resource teacher quietly opens the door for Jack, Billy, and Tabatha to re-enter their fifth-grade class from their special education class. Tabatha heads for a round table at which two other girls are working on their spelling and handwriting assignments while Ms. Wilson leads a discussion in the first of the three reading groups that meet each morning.

"What else did we learn about the use of these plants, Jesse?"

"Each one represents a season, like a season of the year."

Tabatha extracts a paper from her large pink canvas bag and deposits it in a cardboard box lid designated for completed classwork. She walks to her locker behind Ms. Wilson and removes a book stuffed with papers which immediately fall to the floor. Tabatha quickly looks at Ms. Wilson to see if the noise has disturbed the group. Ms. Wilson smiles at her and puts her finger to her lips, silently reminding her that there are to be no disruptions during reading group time. Tabatha gathers up the papers, crams them back into her book, and quietly closes the locker door. She hurries back to her seat, next to the rectangular table at which Billy alternately works on his spelling and talks quietly with another boy.

"Prove it by the text," Ms. Wilson reminds the readers who are guessing at the answer to her question.

Tabatha continues to rummage in her pink bag, periodically stopping as if to rest, and then beginning again. She pulls out three spiral notebooks, stuffing loose papers back into each one. She selects a blue notebook, glances at the clock—9:24—and begins writing. Another girl, hugging a large stuffed panda bear, leaves the reading corner to return to her seat at Tabatha's table. She takes an orange and an apple brought for ten o'clock snack time out of her book bag, selects the apple, and drops the orange back into her bag. She tucks her foot underneath her, rocks back on the legs of her chair, and opens her workbook.

"What does a test of courage make you think of, Doug?"

"It reminds me of a long time ago, it would be like in the Roman times. . . ."

"Oh, okay, you think it's going to be historical fiction. Any other ideas?"

A tall African-American girl who looks older than the other students pushes back her chair and moves slowly toward the reading corner. She drops down on the carpet in front of the bookcase and begins to look over the titles of the books. Three of the windows are opened to the warm April air. The sound of lumber dropping from the construction outside goes unnoticed. At one of the tables beside the windows a girl, dressed like most of the students in jeans and tennis shoes, leisurely picks the wood away from the point of her pencil with her fingernail before taking out notebook paper and beginning to write.

The two boys at her table suddenly look up and close their workbooks. Three students in the reading corner quickly return to their respective tables while Billy, Jack, Tabatha, and Michelle move toward the reading table as the students in the first group prepare to leave it. Two other students stop by Ms. Wilson's desk to pick up their passes before leaving the room for the library. Doug slams his locker door shut, after exchanging one book for another. Another child sharpens her pencil while talking with Jack, who has just placed his spelling paper in the cardboard lid reserved for completed assignments.

Peter, the last member of this second reading group, arrives from his Chapter One class and joins the other Frontiers group members at the reading table. Ms. Wilson moves purposefully toward her chair positioned in the indentation of the kidney-shaped table.

> Reading group time is so important to the children. They get real upset if something happens that they miss their reading group time. I think the reason they feel special about it is because we're in a small group, and they know they're getting a lot of individual attention, even though the group might have seven or eight people. But we're all focused together, and it's one of the few times during the day where they get to really express themselves and where they get to be listened to carefully. I think they really thrive on feeling like what they have to say is important . . . They need opportunities to perform, and this is the one time during the day that they know is theirs and that no other student in another group can interfere with that time.

While the students in the reading group settle into their seats, Tabatha works undistracted by the noise, determined to finish her story so Ms. Wilson can type it that night. Ms. Wilson says, "Today we're going to start a new group of stories that begin on page 137 where there are some children skiing downhill." The students thumb through the pages while Ms. Wilson displays the correct page and repeats the page number again and again until they all have found it.

Ms. Wilson comments, "These are going to be stories about achieving," as she writes the word *achieving* in orange Magic Marker at the top of the large chart pad beside her.

"Now, what does *achieving* mean? [pause, no response] What does it mean? [pause, no answer] If you are achieving, what are you doing?"

"Learning," Jack volunteers.

Ms. Wilson repeats *learning* as she prints it on the chart. "What else?"

A girl leaves her independent seatwork and approaches Ms. Wilson with a paper in hand. She continues to wait as Ms. Wilson questions the group members and listens intently to their answers and comments. Michelle sees the girl and thinks to herself, "Ms. Wilson doesn't want to be disturbed when we are in reading group." After about five minutes, the girl walks to the back of the room and deposits her paper in the cardboard lid.

Tabatha shifts in her chair, shuffles several papers. The noise attracts Ms. Wilson's attention, and she muses:

> She's moving papers around again. She can be working on her handwriting or her spelling and still keep her place in the story. . . Handwriting is a very difficult task for her so she has a tendency to just constantly be working on it . . . even if it's during reading group . . . She never loses her place in the story [though].

Tabatha thinks to herself:

> Because we go to resource, we don't have time to do our work so . . . I do my work when I'm in reading group. I stop and turn the reading book to the right page, and then she (Ms. Wilson) tells me what number, and so I read it. Then after I finish with that page, I go back to the other work.

Billy removes his jacket. Although it's only 9:30, the room already is very warm.

"What is another meaning of 'achieving'?," Ms. Wilson asks.

"Accepting responsibility," Jack offers.

"Wow!" Ms. Wilson exclaims.

Michelle claps.

"Why is she clapping?" Jack asks.

"Because she thought it was so good, she gave you a round of applause. . . Someone else tell me what 'achieving' means?"

She poses the question repeatedly, recording the responses on the chart: "getting good grades", "taking a challenge to do something new."

"All right, let's look at the stories and see if we get ideas of what 'achieving' means. . . . Lots of times you can tell just from the title and the pictures."

Ms. Wilson notes key phrases that describe achievement as the students find them in the stories in this unit. A petite girl, whose mussed hair and purple flowered slacks suggest she has not as yet adopted the concern for appearance and uniform dress exhibited by most of the students in the class, glances toward the front of the room. Her eyes rest on the long narrow bulletin board which runs across the top of the chalkboard. Here students' batik pictures are displayed, separating laminated sheets of construction paper upon which the class rules are neatly written in Magic Marker:

> Use a quiet voice when you might distract others with a loud voice.
>
> Sit still by being in your seat with your arms and legs to yourself.
>
> Do careful work by reading the directions, writing neatly, and checking it over.
>
> Do not use a loud voice to announce things to the class that only concern you or a few others.
>
> When it is someone's turn to talk, don't interrupt.
>
> Don't avoid doing your work by procrastinating . . . looking around . . . sharpening pencils . . .going to the restroom . . . walking around, etc.
>
> Don't disturb others who are doing their work.
>
> Work independently by doing your work all by yourself.
>
> Wait for help by sitting quietly and working on something else.

Ms. Wilson glances at each of the students in the reading group as if taking a mental inventory and thinks:

> Peter hasn't been participating. I want to bring him into the group and get him to focus on the story. I want to help him participate, to become a part of the group.

"Would you read the lead-in, Peter?"

After he finishes reading, Ms. Wilson says, "Good, Peter. Can you tell us where this mountain is?" Getting no response, she asks, "Would you like to choose a helper?" As Peter thinks about whom he will choose, Ms. Wilson muses:

> Choosing a helper really works. If a child can't remember or can't find the answer in the text, rather than give up or say, "I don't know," I'd rather he'd choose a helper. In doing that, he listens to the person he has chosen. If I chose someone else to answer, he'd tune me out, but he won't tune out one of his peers.

Peter selects Jack to be his helper, and Jack gives the correct response.

Ms. Wilson says, "What part of the climb was the most dangerous? [pause, no response] This is where we finished yesterday. You've read this."

"The narrow part," one of the students says.

"The narrow part. What other part was dangerous?"

Two boys who are in the seatwork group raise their hands to answer the question. Getting no response from the reading group members, Ms. Wilson sends the students back to the text to find the answer. Michelle announces she's found the answer, but Ms. Wilson tells her to wait, thinking:

> I know she's ready to answer, but I have to wait and give the others a chance to find it. If I go ahead and call on her at this moment, the others would immediately quit.

Ms. Wilson nods at Billy, the next child in the circle, signaling him to begin reading aloud. She supplies words which he has difficulty decoding. "All right, Billy, what two good things happened?" As Billy answers, Ms. Wilson thinks:

> I directed the question to him and not to any other student. I don't want to open it up for discussion. Billy has a problem with short-term and long-term memory. He can decode the words, but he has no comprehension. So I want to, very quickly, right as he's finishing his reading, to get him to zero back in on what he has learned from it. I'm not sure if Tabatha is listening.

"Tabatha, what two things happened in Billy's paragraph?"

Jack calls out part of the answer.

"Let her talk. Tabatha, why was using the oxygen good? [long pause] Would you like to choose a helper?"

"Yes. Billy."

After Billy gives the correct response, Ms. Wilson asks Tabatha to repeat the answer in her own words and then moves on to the next student in the group.

"Jack, will you read next?"

Reading slowly, word by word, he skips a line. Ms. Wilson reaches over to his book and places a strip of green paper under the omitted line as a marker. She thinks,

He needs a line across there. He's really beginning to get frustrated.

As Jack continues to read, Ms. Wilson snaps her fingers at two students in the reading corner who are talking. They quickly stop chatting and begin again to concentrate on their books. Jack continues to read. Billy doodles on his workbook cover. Suddenly Tabatha stops swinging her legs and leans forward. It's her turn to read.

Ms. Wilson asks her, "Are the two sentences the same or different: 'The dog was black with white spots. The dog was white with black spots'?"

Tabatha smiles at Ms. Wilson. Two other students are eager to answer.

"Let her think. She's thinking. That's wonderful."

"Different," Tabatha answers hesitantly.

"Can you draw a picture to show me how they are different?"

Tabatha smiles shyly at the other group members.

"Oh, I got it wrong," Billy blurts out.

"Tabatha's going to show you how they're different."

Tabatha takes the Magic Marker somewhat reluctantly. "I can't draw dogs."

"It doesn't matter," Ms. Wilson assures her. "We understand. First of all, you're going to draw me a dog that's black with white spots."

Michelle stretches so she can see around Ms. Wilson. Billy smiles, seeming to enjoy the event vicariously. As Tabatha finishes the second drawing, she thinks:

> It helps me to see that one of the dogs had black spots and one of the dogs had white spots and that *'different'* was the right answer and *'same'* wasn't.

"Billy, you said you got this one wrong. Are these dogs the same or different?"

"Different."

"This is the same thing we've done in math. Remember sometimes in math when we need to solve a problem, we said it helps to draw a picture. Doesn't it really help you here?"

"Yes," the children answer in unison.

"I love the pictures," Ms. Wilson comments to the children as she thinks to herself:

One of the things that I feel real strongly about in teaching is that children learn how to think, and I try to word my questions so they are required to think on a little higher level. Being able to tell how something is different is a higher-level type of thinking, and these children are capable of doing that.

"Billy, go." Billy begins his reading turn. Ms. Wilson's head jerks upward. She stares over the heads of the group members toward the reading corner and snaps her fingers to get the talker's attention. She then points from the reading corner to the student's chair, thinking:

Several children have gotten into the reading corner which is their place to read, but they're not reading. They're talking to each other, and it's beginning to disturb me and distract me; and so rather than say anything, I try to use a lot of nonverbal behaviors.

"Billy, are those two sentences the same or different?"
Billy looks at Michelle.
"Don't be looking at her for the answer. Think for yourself."
Tabatha smiles, and thinks to herself:

Ms. Wilson wants him to figure it out for himself.

Michelle nods and also thinks:

He's gotta know it by himself.

Ms. Wilson reasons:

I think it's probably another characteristic of this type of student. They look for clues from other people or from the teacher. He knows he's not going to get many clues from me, so he's trying to get clues from other students.

"Would you like to choose a helper?" she asks. Ms. Wilson glances up at the clock. It's 9:45 already.
"Jack, it's your turn." As Jack reads, Ms. Wilson reflects:

He's having difficulty reading today. At times he can read very well and very fluently. At other times he can't focus on the page, and he can't get the letter to make sense to him. He tries really hard, or he has tried in the past really hard to sound out the words; and I've tried to get him away from that because I know he does not have comfortable decoding skills. So I've taught him to read the words that he can and to bump the other words and continue on.

Jack slaps his fist on the table and says, "I'm reading awful."

"That's all right. Sometimes you just have to get your mind going. . . . Don't you want to go back to 'onto our backs' and see if you can read it from there?"

"Where's 'onto our back'?"

"After 'these iron plates prevent slipping.'"

Jack rereads that portion of the story and finishes the passage with difficulty. Ms. Wilson claps as she thinks to herself:

Just a few minutes ago, he was having a very difficult time. . . . but he went back to it, and he tried again which made me very proud of him. . . . He remembered a strategy that I've used with him . . . If you don't get a word, go back and read the whole sentence and see if you can figure it out, and he did and he figured it out.

She asks, "What was dangerous about the climb?" Getting no response to this question, Ms. Wilson directs them back to the text to find the answer and considers:

I've tried to stress with them all year to just not be guessing at answers, because this type of group of children has a tendency to just guess at everything, and they also have a tendency to latch on to some response that another kid has given, even though that response is incorrect. So I'm trying to get them to think for themselves, and I'm also trying to show them how they can think for themselves by going to the text and proving it from the text.

She says, "Tabatha, why are you working way back at the beginning of the workbook? I'm proud of your wanting to work on these pages, but right now I'd like you to stay with us where we are."

Ms. Wilson reassures herself:

I had to let her know, well, it's fine to practice these pages, and they can do that on their own time; but right now I'd like her to stay with us in our skill lesson.

"Would you like to read?" Mrs. Wilson asks.

Tabatha begins to read and has difficulty decoding the word *periscope*. Ms. Wilson says, "Periscope," and immediately outlines a periscope on the drawing of a submarine she had sketched earlier on the chart pad. She thinks to herself:

> I feel that as many visual, auditory, concrete clues that are gonna help them learn . . . I'm gonna try to do as many of them as I can. They're going to have to learn through every means possible. So I try to remember to do those things.

Ms. Wilson checks the time—9:55. It's almost time for the reading group to end and snack time to begin. Kim, the young child of one of Ms. Wilson's parent volunteers enters the room and runs over to sit on her lap.

"Billy," she asks, "could you tell Kim what our story's about?"

As Billy reviews the highlights of the story, Ms. Wilson thinks:

> I summarize, or let the children summarize, every day. Today I let the children summarize for Kim, and I'll summarize just the theme of the story. . . . I also like for them to look forward to tomorrow. Hopefully they might think about it a little bit, or they might try to sneak a peek . . . If they do that, all the better for them because they need all the advantages they can get . . . If I sort of tell them what we're going to do tomorrow, at least they know what they've got to look forward to and what to expect the next day in class. I don't want them to feel surprised or feel that what we're going to be doing might be threatening or too hard for them.

"Before group ends I need your worksheets," Ms. Wilson announces.

All members except two boys hand in their papers. She asks Billy and Jack when they can finish the work. They agree to have their sheets done by math time.

Jack asks if he can help Peter with his story for the class newspaper. Ms. Wilson denies the request while acknowledging his good intentions. She reminds herself:

> Having knowledge of my children helps. Jack would like for me to let him help Peter, but they would be doing more socialization . . . So rather than saying, "Naw, you'll just misbehave or something," I try to give him a reason why Peter needs to work by himself and not put him [Jack] down . . . I try to let him think that that was nice of you to ask, but at this moment, I'd like for Peter to think about it himself. I didn't . . . reject his offer.

QUESTIONS FOR REFLECTION

• How would you characterize Joyce's teaching? What models of instruction or teaching approaches does she emphasize?

• What outcomes does Joyce value for the students in this reading group? Are these desirable for students with learning disabilities? Why or why not? Would the outcomes you pursue be similar or different?

• What do you think about the use of this reading group as part of the plan for integrating Joyce's special education students in her classroom? What do you see as the potential benefits and drawbacks of this instructional choice?

THEMES THAT SHAPE JOYCE'S TEACHING

We now discuss the eight themes, or patterns of thinking and behaving, we identified from our observations of Joyce Wilson's teaching and our interviews with her. We illustrate our descriptions with examples of classroom events.

Promoting Individual Thinking

Many instances in our observations suggest that Ms. Wilson believes it is important for students to think for themselves. She prompts and provides opportunities for them to think independently. For example, when one student gave an incorrect answer, she provided several clues to the correct response. The children, however, continued to accept and repeat the incorrect answer. She explained to the students that they all were incorrect because they had "latched on" to the first answer given rather than think the problem through for themselves. She admonished them not to "follow the pack" but to "use their own minds."

Promoting Students' Self-Concept

During our visits to Ms. Wilson's classroom, we noted how she strongly emphasizes the children's need to feel good about themselves. She speaks and acts in ways that promote her students' self-concepts. An instance of this theme occurred when one of her students brought in his drawing which was based on a movie and story the group had seen and read earlier in the week. Ms. Wilson praised him, first for doing something extra on his own initiative and second for combining information from both the movie and story sources in his drawing.

Using Rules and Routines

The routine procedures of the classroom allow Ms. Wilson to focus almost exclusively on reading instruction with a group of students while her other students work independently. She establishes and enforces rules and routines as management procedures that maximize instructional time and/or productivity for everyone. For example, students moved through the schedule, depositing completed papers in the appropriate place, picking up library passes at the correct time, and beginning and ending work activities almost in unison without reminders from her. To outsiders like us, the classroom seemed to run on automatic pilot.

Engaging in Nonverbal Behaviors

As one of the ways to enforce classroom rules and routines, Ms. Wilson frequently uses nonverbal behaviors to focus student attention and maximize instructional time. For example, she put her finger to her lips to silence a student who talked out during the reading group, snapped her fingers to quiet those outside the group, and indicated that a talker in the reading corner should return to her seat by pointing first at the student and then at her chair. Like an orchestra leader who signals each player with the baton, Ms. Wilson silently directed her students' movements and behaviors.

Holding Children Accountable

We identified this as a salient theme after observing Ms. Wilson's efforts to make students responsible for participating in the learning process. The theme is apparent, for instance, in her expectations that students complete their homework and in her encouragement of participation in group discussions.

Choosing a Helper

We often saw Ms. Wilson suggest that students select a peer to provide assistance when they did not know the correct response. Recall that she asked Peter if he wanted to choose a helper when he could not answer her question. She sees this as a technique to help students stay engaged in the activities while supporting their needs and self-concepts.

Providing Visual Examples of Concepts

Two instances from our description of a typical day display Ms. Wilson's awareness of the need to represent concepts in multiple ways. First, she asked Tabatha to draw pictures that represented two sentences to help clarify the concepts of same and different. Second, after Tabatha had difficulty decoding the word "periscope," she pronounced the word, quickly sketched a periscope, and wrote the word above the drawing. Ms. Wilson's provision of visual clues serves the purpose of increasing instructional opportunities for the students.

Questioning

It is interesting to note that, although Ms. Wilson uses questioning as the primary instructional technique during the reading group, she does not indicate that it is central to her role as a teacher. She seems to focus on and feel most passionately about the needs of her students. She does not appear to concentrate on her own instructional behaviors, even the one that she uses most frequently.

CONCLUSION

Joyce Wilson's overriding concern is the emotional and social well-being of her students. She knows each child's individual needs, both because she observes them carefully in school and because she learns firsthand about their lives outside of school. To her, "math and other school subjects are not as important as getting [them] to work with other people and to feel good about [themselves]."

At the same time, she understands that the reading group time is important to the children. It is "the one time during the day that they know is theirs and that no other student . . . can interfere." The classroom routines which Ms. Wilson has established allow other students to function independently while she leads each of the groups. At first glance, the constant movement of the students to the reading corner, to the library, to turn in completed assignments seems like quiet confusion. A longer, closer look, however, reveals that the students' movements are efficient and purposeful, part of Ms. Wilson's plan to keep the classroom running smoothly, the students involved, and the instructional time uninterrupted. Her concern for her students' social and emotional welfare, coupled with the rules and routines she establishes, creates "an atmosphere where we are working together and care about each other."

QUESTIONS FOR REFLECTION

- Which of the themes that describe Joyce's teaching would you choose to emulate? Why are they important to you? How would you realize them in your classroom?

- Which of the themes do you think are the most useful for supporting the successful inclusion of students with learning disabilities into general education classroom? How do they help meet the needs of special education students? How do they connect with research-supported instructional techniques that facilitate integration?

CHAPTER 6

Anne North: "I Try to Provide Them with the Correct Model"

Jean S. Lindsay
University of Virginia

Edward A. McShane
University of Virginia

Anne North, a special education teacher in a rural school about 12 miles from Charter Hills, was selected as the subject of this case study because she had been identified as an outstanding student in her master's program in special education. We sought to enhance our understanding of teachers who work with students with learning disabilities who are integrated in regular classrooms by studying how a successful teacher works with these students in a self-contained, special education setting.

THE COMMUNITY AND THE SCHOOL

At the time of our study, Anne North was teaching in an elementary school located in a rural center near Charter Hills. The little town, with its scattering of shops and its single supermarket, is surrounded by farms and apple and peach orchards. On the edge of the town is its largest industry, a food processing plant that employs local workers, many of whom live on farms, in isolated houses on country roads, or on the quiet, tree-shaded streets of the town. A number of young professionals who prefer its rural flavor and appreciate its lower housing costs have also been attracted to the town.

Johnson Elementary School, where Ms. North teaches, is located on the edge of town. The school's small, old, brick building with its warm, homey quality was replaced by a more modern structure across the street the year after we finished our work in Ms. North's classroom. The student population is quite homogeneous, with only a few students coming from professional families and only a few African-American students in the school. Most of the students come from lower middle-class working or farm families. Some live in pockets of rural poverty and unemployment.

Ms. North's small classroom is downstairs, across from the furnace room and a little "out of the mainstream" of the school. One side of the room holds desks arranged in orderly rows. Here she conducts lessons and activities for the whole class. A kidney-shaped table with one chair in its center and four or five chairs around it is used when she teaches smaller groups. The other half of the room contains a large round table with chairs around it and two large desks, one for Ms. North, the other for her aide. Here students do individual activities with the aide. A bookshelf stands perpendicular to the wall and forms a corner labeled "Quiet Area." There are some pillows on the floor, and in this area students can relax and read during their free time. A computer sits in the back right corner of the room.

At the front of the room is a blackboard where Ms. North writes the day and date and a list of five tasks the students must do. Each day she reviews the items and gives any special instructions. Near her accustomed place at the board is an easel which contains lists of the target words for that day and new concepts she is introducing. Along the left wall is a bulletin board labeled "Our Good Work" where the students' work is displayed. Another board on the right wall holds a calendar surrounded with cutout theme pictures.

Along the right wall is another table, referred to as "the learning center," where folders are kept with work for each student to complete. Over the table are three posters which list some of the rules and systems for the class. The first describes "How to Earn Points" and is divided into two categories, one for behavior and another for grades. The second poster keeps a tally of these points and reads, "Did I Earn Friday Fun Time?" It shows the number of points each student has earned each day and the weekly total needed to get the free fun time on Friday afternoon. The third poster is a schedule for using the learning center table.

THE TEACHER

Anne North has made teaching her second career. She practiced law for 10 years before becoming a teacher. Her decision to become a teacher grew out of her dislike for the confrontational aspect of the legal profession. In her work with Legal Aid, she had learned that she liked work that involved helping low-income people.

In high school Ms. North had wanted to be a teacher, but when she finished college she felt that "somehow teaching didn't seem to have enough prestige." When she decided to pursue a profession other than the law, "teaching recurred as something I would enjoy doing." The area of special education offered the opportunity to pursue her interest in "how people learn." She lived near a state university which had a teacher preparation program, and she decided to pursue a master's program that would prepare her for dual certification to teach students either with learning disabilities or with emotional/behavioral disorders.

After Ms. North completed her master's degree, she and her husband moved to Alaska. There she taught students in a primary-level, self-contained special education class. Though the students had a variety of problems, they were all working on the same skills, and she was able to group them together for instruction. She found that she enjoyed teaching. When she returned to Charter Hills, she found a position at a private school known for its highly structured approach toward teaching students with learning disabilities.

The next year she was hired to teach students with learning disabilities in a self-contained setting at Johnson Elementary. The year after our study Ms. North became the teacher in that school's resource room for students with learning disabilities and emotional/behavioral disorders.

THE STUDENTS

Our first impression of Ms. North's class focused on its great diversity. The class contains 11 children of widely varying size whose ages range from 7 through 13. Although it is called a self-contained class for students with learning disabilities, it includes two students labeled as emotionally/behaviorally disordered who are being re-evaluated. One of them, resembling a child with learning disabilities with severe language and organizational difficulties, is possibly autistic. The other seems clearly autistic, and Ms. North believes he is misplaced in her classroom.

Ms. North describes the range of her students' needs this way:

> I have three children who are fifth-grade age . . . who are working
> anywhere from the second- to the fourth-grade level. I have four
> fourth-graders who are all working on a second-grade level. I have
> one third-grader who is working, probably about at first-grade level.
> Then I have two second graders, one of whom is working on a first-
> grade level and one who's working probably on a kindergarten level.
> No serious behavior problems other than just hyperactive stuff,
> except for the autistic child, who has some self-stimulatory behavior,
> nothing real serious. He's not really very well toilet-trained,
> echolalic, nonresponsive, mostly just kind of sits and does nothing,
> unless you're directly there pushing him, and he's the only behavior
> problem, I'd say.

Because all the children were identified for special education
services in some way, we did not identify a single, target child as had
been done in the other case studies.

A TYPICAL LESSON IN MS. NORTH'S CLASSROOM

During the first half hour of the school day, the students in Ms. North's
room are expected to get organized for the day, go over their
assignments from their general education classes, meet with Ms. North
to check on these assignments, and work independently. At 8:40 the
last two students come in and take their places at their desks. Most of
the students are working, although there is quite a bit of talking. Several
students are at the back table with Mrs. Winston, the aide.

Ms. North, from her desk, asks who has brought picture money and
takes care of a couple of other housekeeping matters. The students still
keep working on their own. They often move around, for example, to
turn in work, ask Ms. North a question, and obtain materials. While
there continues to be talking back and forth, it is pretty low-key and the
room seems well-controlled. After checking the work of several
students and apparently finding that some work has not been done, Ms.
North says to the class as a whole, in a sort of spontaneous pep talk,
"I'll give you all the help I can . . . but I need some help from you." Ms.
North passes out stars to the several students who have completed all
their homework. Now she looks over at several students who are
completing worksheets and says, "Make sure you read all the

directions. The reason I give you things like this is to see if you can follow directions."

At three minutes to nine, Ms. North, seated at her desk, says, "I need people seated at their desks unless Mrs. Winston is working with you." She tells Sean to clear his work off his desk and then tells everyone to put pencils down. They respond fairly quickly as Ms. North rises from her desk, moves to the front of the room, and waits for them to be ready. She says, "Good, everyone showed good listening behaviors."

She begins the lesson with what is obviously a daily routine. "Today is Monday, October thirteenth," she says then goes over a list of tasks on the board for them to work on during the day. Next she says that they will do "something new" and points out that the writing on the board today is in cursive. She tells them that they will be working on cursive writing at the learning center table. They all have centers to visit today, and they are to do the center activity that is listed by number after their names on the poster above the learning center table.

Ms. North reminds them that there is a fourth-grade field trip tomorrow and that four of them will be going on that trip. She reminds the three students who are integrated into general education classes in the afternoon that they are to work on certain materials first. Through all these instructions, the class remains well-focused on Ms. North. She speaks slowly and distinctly and pauses from time to time to make sure that they are all with her. She seems very thorough in highlighting the specifics of their requirements. The work is well-organized, clear, and straightforward. Each student seems to know what is expected of him.

Mrs. North says, "Okay, last thing," and moves to the easel in the left front of the room. She reintroduces a list of vowel teams and sample words. She puts her hand beside the first word and says, "Get ready." As she goes through the list, cueing them with her hand, they respond in unison. When the group has read aloud all the words, she begins to call on individual students. First she calls on a boy who does not have his hand up and then on two who do have their hands up. All three make it through the list successfully. As each one finishes, Ms. North says, "Pat yourself on the back."

She gives some examples of vowel team words and calls on the students one at a time to repeat them. Ronnie has not been paying attention for a minute or two, and now he is turned all the way around in his seat, looking at the boy behind him. In a matter-of-fact tone, Ms.

North tells him to turn around and goes on with the lesson. A minute later she says again, "Ronnie, you're not turned around."

She finishes the lesson and then says, "Okay, points." She moves around the class telling each student how many points to give himself. They keep their own daily tally, with 90 points out of a possible 100 needed to earn a treat each day. Most of the students get 10 points this time; Ronnie and one other get only 9, and Ms. North tells each of them why. To Ronnie she says, "I had to tell you to turn around."

The students, especially Ronnie and the other boy who got nine, grumble a bit and say things like, "He was talking, too." Ms. North ignores them. When Sean tells her that Ronnie was doing something with his pencil, she responds in the same matter-of-fact tone she used with Ronnie, "Yes, but you were participating in it."

Now Ms. North calls the first reading group up to her table. These are the younger students—Michael, Ronnie, John, and Matt. They move to the table quickly and without much noise. The rest of the students settle down to work, either at their desks or at the back table with the aide. As soon as the four boys sit down, Ms. North tells them to put down their pencils. She has to repeat this individually to Ronnie.

She starts the lesson quickly by telling them to open their spelling books and repeat a set of letters after her. Her instructions are fast-paced, but the students all seem to follow her. She says, "Get ready," and has them go through the list of letters in unison. As usual, she uses hand signals, with her palm turned alternately toward them and away from them, to cue them to respond. Satisfied with their performance on the letters, she promptly moves to a list of words in the spelling book.

Ms. North first has the students say the whole word together, then one part of it, then the whole word again: for example, "*cannot, can, cannot.*" She proceeds quickly, generating many responses from them. They finish the list of words and Ms. North immediately gives directions for the next activity. As she talks, she hands out tokens for the first part of the lesson. She is very adept with the tokens and hands them out almost automatically. She says, "This time, try to answer right on signal." Matt and John, she says, were right on it, but Ronnie and Michael were a little behind. Again, she tells Ronnie and Michael to work on responding right at the signal.

Now Ms. North tells the group to read the word she is pointing to "the fast way" and then to sound it out. All four are able to read the word *wanted* but mumble when they break it into two parts. The pattern of Matt and John being right on the signal continues. They are a little more sure of the words, and Ronnie and Michael follow their lead.

Ms. North tells Ronnie to sit up and speak louder, adding that she cannot hear him. He does not respond. She looks at him and repeats her request. Still getting no response, she goes on with the lesson. Matt and John are really involved in the activity, Michael is following along, and Ronnie is participating less and less.

At 9:15 they finish this part of the lesson, and Ms. North hands out more tokens. She tells Ronnie, "No smile this time; you weren't doing it with us." She starts to move quickly to the next activity but then notices that Ronnie is not paying attention. She stops and gives him a little pep talk. She uses a gentle tone but tells him straightforwardly what she expects. She says she needs two things from him: to see his mouth move and to hear him. She tries to coax a response from him but gets none.

Now Ms. North passes out reading books to the four boys and has them read the instructions for a game they are going to play. They read in unison, one word at a time; and when they have reached the end of each sentence, she has them read the whole sentence again. When they finish reading, she asks them several questions, using a scripted lesson which she has in front of her, thinking:

> I need to be sure they know what they are supposed to do. The questions are to check on that.

She plays the game with them. They have to stand up, touch the floor, and sit down. Then she quickly changes to the story. She is moving the activities at a very rapid pace, but her students seem to keep up with her and pay attention.

They start the story in unison, again reading each word and then the whole sentence. After they read the whole sentence together, Ms. North repeats it. She taps her pencil to pace them for each word, and they read in a monotone. After doing a few sentences in this way, she has them read individually. She calls on Ronnie first, and he reads well. She praises him enthusiastically saying, "Good job!" They all read fairly well. Michael has the least expression, but he completes his sentence.

While Ms. North is working with this group, two students, Carrie and Denny, are at the back table with Mrs. Winston, the aide. Sean and Chris are working on their own. Paul starts and stops continually. Each time he stops working, he smiles and looks around the room. He is writing first with one hand and then with the other. Steve just sits and stares in the direction of Ms. North's table.

After each of the four boys has read, Ms. North says, "Good job. Now let's go back to the beginning. This time I'm going to ask you some questions." As she gives these instructions, she passes out more tokens to each boy for the preceding part of the lesson; she then moves right into the new activity. They read the title in unison. Ms. North taps out each word, and they read each word separately. She is using the questions in the manual, such as, "What is the story about?" They offer reasonable answers, and she has them start reading one by one. She stops them from time to time to ask questions, and all of them are following along well. When she asks a question, she cues them to wait and then answer all together. The scripted lesson is very methodical and repetitive, but she has them all involved in answering the questions. At times she helps them rephrase their answers so they match the questions from the manual. Ronnie is just as involved as the others.

They finish the lesson, and Ms. North passes out worksheets for them to do at their desks. While the boys are writing their names on the sheets, she figures out how many points each one will get for this lesson and passes out M&M's candies as a reward. John and Matt each get 10 points. Michael gets 9; Ms. North tells him he needs to work on coming in on cue. He says once that he *was* coming in on cue, but she ignores this statement, and he drops the subject. Ronnie gets 7 points and an admonition to "talk up"; he seems to be in a good mood again and does not complain at all. He looks at his M&Ms and says, "How did you know I like green?"

As the first group is leaving, Ms. North calls up the second group, asking them to bring their books and pencils. These are the older students—Chris, Sean, Paul, and Steve. It takes Steve two or three minutes to get out the book he needs, get a pencil, and go over to the table. She starts talking to the other three, but it is obvious that she is waiting for Steve. When he reaches the table, she praises him for having his book and pencil, thinking:

> It is important to me to include Steve in the activities of the class and try to get what I can out of him.

While Ms. North starts working with this group—using the same format she used with the first group but a different book—Michael,

John, and Ronnie cluster around their desks. They talk back and forth as they try to get started on their worksheets. They become fairly noisy, but Ms. North does not respond.

The second group is also reading lists of single words with Ms. North, and all except Steve keep at the expected pace. She says to Steve, "I need your attention." He does not respond. As she is switching to a new activity, she tells John and Michael that they should not be talking and says to Ronnie, "You shouldn't be playing with things." They quiet down.

Ms. North presents some new words with the second group. After she has them read each word, she explains what it means and has them repeat it. Again, she is following a scripted lesson, and she moves through it very quickly. As before, she says, "Get ready," before each response and uses hand cues to set their pace.

After this group introduction to the words, she calls on them individually to read the list. She gives tokens to each one as he finishes. Steve is the first to read. He hesitates for just a second and then haltingly reads three or four words correctly. The other three boys each take a turn and read all the words. Each one gets stuck one or two times, and Ms. North helps him with the word.

They proceed to the next activity of reading sentences. Paul, Sean, and Chris all do quite well. Steve reads very softly, dragging out each word. When they have all had a turn, they go back to the beginning and read the story again, this time with Ms. North asking questions from the manual. The first question is about who the main character is. Sean has to look back into the book to find the answer. When it is Steve's turn, he does not respond. Ms. North tells him the answer and has him repeat it, which he does.

Meanwhile, there continues to be a fair amount of noise in the room. John is trying to work, but Michael interrupts him often to ask for help. This easily turns into play. When Michael reads on his own, he reads out loud; no one seems to notice or be bothered by this. Ronnie goes back to the table where the aide is and starts talking with Carrie and Denny, who are also there. Ms. North looks over and says, "There's a lot of talking at the table back there. Ronnie, are you working or talking? You need to work with your mouth closed."

The reading group with Ms. North finishes, and she reviews for them. She tells them to put away their books and open their workbooks. She explains the directions step-by-step with them and reminds them that they need to have a check for each item. She repeats: "Direction number one is. . ." She asks, "What is direction number one?" She calls on Paul to answer, and he starts to read the first question. "No," she says, "I mean *direction* number one."

After they finish reviewing the directions, they start on the questions. She takes them through the answers to the first few, but for the rest she only gives them hand cues. A few times she has to tell someone the answer, and she immediately has him repeat it. She thinks:

> That's the procedure to correct. You tell them the answer and then have them repeat it.

She has them complete one more exercise in their workbooks before ending the lesson. As usual, she moves them quickly through it, using cues to help them. A recurring theme of these exercises is the constant review of what they have just done.

Having finished with the second group, Ms. North sends them to their seats and quickly begins to get ready for the next direct instruction activity of the day.

QUESTIONS FOR REFLECTION

- How would you characterize Anne's teaching? What models of instruction or teaching approaches does she emphasize?

- What outcomes for her special education students might Anne be valuing with these instructional choices? Are some of her values ones you might also choose if you were teaching in her context? Why or why not? What might you do differently if you were the teacher of these students?

- In what ways might Anne's work in her special education classroom support the future integration of her students into general education classrooms? What else would you want to see occur to help with such a transition?

OVERALL FINDINGS

We now discuss four themes, or patterns of thinking and behaving, we identified from our observations of Anne North's teaching and our interviews with her. Several of these themes have multiple components which help define them.

Direct Instruction Techniques and Materials

Ms. North relies heavily on direct instruction approaches. She characterizes this methodology as

> fast-paced, [which] involves keeping a high percentage of responses from all the children. . . . You try to keep all the children involved with the things, and you're aiming at a specific skill. That's what direct instruction is to me.

Ms. North developed a set of routines that helped her implement this teaching approach more easily and that helped her students handle the complexities of this classroom. Once the students had learned the routines, they knew what was expected of them. Many of these routines were associated with a particular set of materials. The corrective reading materials, for example, called for fast-paced, rapid responses to the teachers' cues. Other routines we identified that allowed Ms. North to attend to aspects of her students' performance included monitoring, analyzing, and reviewing; establishing rules and procedures; cuing, drilling, and practicing; checking and correcting; and modeling.

It was interesting to observe Ms. North's teaching behavior when she departed from one of these routines. This happened infrequently, but the following excerpt from a stimulated recall interview illustrates her difficulty when it occurred.

Event: [Ms. North gives a description of bamboo.]

Thought: They really took me by surprise there. I had no idea how to describe bamboo to them, and these children in general have such a limited exposure to things in the world that I often stop and try to explain things like that to them. But I couldn't think of any point of reference. My grandfather raised sugar cane, so I thought maybe the student could relate to sugar cane. It was clear that he didn't know what cane was. So I don't think he got the point. I should have just pointed to the picture and said that's what it looks like.

All of the components of Ms. North's direct instruction approach supported what was a core objective for her: to teach her students the skills and strategies that they lacked. In a stimulated recall interview, she mentioned 20 such skills, ranging from teaching a child with autism how to use a tissue when he sneezed to teaching reading comprehension.

Relating Research Findings to Instruction

As a second theme, Ms. North frequently uses the research literature to inform her teaching.

> I read a lot in journals, and particularly *Exceptional Children*, and so I pick up a lot of things that I do from reading journals. If I run across—well, like last year when I taught in another school, I didn't know how to teach reading comprehension, so I went back through journals and found articles and basically had the direct instruction focus I was looking for: techniques that broke skills down and specifically taught skills as opposed to directed listening, thinking activities, which I like.

Knowledge about Students' Characteristics

Ms. North's knowledge of learner characteristics is derived from two sources. One consists of the courses about characteristics of exceptional children which she has taken at the university; the other is her experience teaching exceptional children. In our interviews, Ms. North frequently refers to the kind of exceptionality of each child and to the kinds of behaviors that characterize that particular exceptionality. For instance:

> He was still not participating in any of the unison responses . . . . He was clearly aware of what was going on, and when I called on him, he was able to make a relevant, appropriate comment in most cases. So, I thought he did a real nice job of participating. Maybe it is possible to integrate an autistic child into a learning disabilities class.

Many times Ms. North appeals to individuals or offers them additional instruction or private praise, as she is aware of the kinds of tasks each student is able to perform and those with which they have difficulty.

Effects of the Setting

Even though Ms. North is characterized as an expert teacher, she believes she cannot always do her best teaching in this setting. Four major constraints affect her teaching.

The earlier description of the diversity of her students and their learning needs indicates one of the obstacles Ms. North has to overcome in order to bring structure to her class. In one interview, she told us:

> I have three children with very disparate abilities; and if I had a more homogeneous class, I would not group these three children together. So, it's one of the constraints that's placed upon me by the composition of the class ... and ... I am not happy with the results ... but I have not been able to figure out a solution for it.

A second constraint of the setting occurred when Ms. North took over the class from a previous teacher and inherited her classroom structures and arrangements.

> I'm in an odd situation because this class has been here. I'm the only person who's new in the class. The aide was here, all the children were here, [laughs] and then I came into the class ... So it's been sort of an interesting experience, trying to fit in. It's kind of like substitute teacher syndrome. They're always telling me, "We don't do it that way in here."

The way her students are integrated into general education classrooms represents a third factor affecting Ms. North's teaching situation. The students vary in the degree to which they are mainstreamed into regular classrooms. They are all mainstreamed for gym and music. One of them is mainstreamed during the entire afternoon for science and social studies, and one of the younger children is mainstreamed for science. Ms. North sees a certain irony in the fact that her students are placed in a self-contained class because they are not making it in the regular class, and yet the constant pressure to integrate has prevented some students from receiving all of the potential benefits of a self-contained classroom.

The fourth constraint that affects Ms. North's teaching situation is the regular curriculum. She is charged with teaching from these materials whenever possible. The goal of the school administration is to return students in self-contained classes to their regular classrooms as soon as possible. Therefore, if students test at grade level in any subject, Ms. North is expected to use the regular curriculum with them. For example, in a math lesson we observed, she used the math book from the regular curriculum.

CONCLUSION

The routines Anne North selects are a response to the special kind of class she teaches. Her preservice training and her in-service experience lead her to expect that children with learning problems will function best in a structured setting. She has learned from the research literature and her own experience that direct instruction leads to higher learning outcomes than other instructional approaches. She has integrated this teaching method with behaviorist classroom management techniques to produce her own set of routines that help her meet the goal of teaching her students the skills and strategies they need. These routines are especially important for her because of the constraints she faces in her teaching situation.

QUESTIONS FOR REFLECTION

- Which of the themes that describe Anne's teaching do you see as valuable for your own teaching? Why are they important to you?

- How can these themes, generated through teaching in a special education classroom, inform ways of successfully including students with disabilities in general education classrooms?

CHAPTER 7

Courtney Littleton: "I Haven't Really Decided What I Think I Should Do about That"

Mary Phillips Manke
Mankato State University

Antony D. Norman
Western Kentucky University

During this project, Courtney Littleton was a student teacher in a fifth-grade classroom in one of the elementary schools in Charter Hills. We chose to observe Ms. Littleton specifically because she was a student teacher. Since she had little teaching experience, we thought her work with students mainstreamed into her classroom might differ from that of the experienced teachers, known to be effective, who were the subjects of the other four case studies in this series.

THE COMMUNITY AND THE SCHOOL

Approximately 4,500 students attend the public schools of Charter Hills. Prior to the year when Ms. Littleton did her student teaching, concerns for equal education in the city led to a reorganization of the system so that neighborhood elementary schools serve only students in kindergarten through fourth grade. All fifth- and sixth-grade students attend one school, renamed Grove Upper Elementary School, and all seventh- and eighth-grade students attend another.

Reorganization made this a year of change for everyone at Grove School. All of the students are new to the school since both the fifth-

and sixth-graders had attended their neighborhood elementary schools the previous year. Over half of the teachers have moved to Grove from a neighborhood school or are newly hired. Also, the school has grown in numbers with the change. Nearly 600 students are in attendance, and every classroom in the school is full.

According to the teachers at the school, a high priority in assigning students to teachers and teaching teams is to ensure that students from all of the neighborhood schools are mixed in every classroom. As a result, students are grouped by achievement, contrary to previous practices in the school system, which has a tradition of at least semi-heterogeneous grouping. Ms. Littleton is assigned to a class made up primarily of low-achieving students. Some are reading on grade level, but many are not.

Crowded and cluttered, the classroom where Ms. Littleton teaches had been a science classroom when Grove was a middle school, and about one-third of the space is occupied by three permanently fixed lab tables with sinks. Ms. Arden, Ms. Littleton's supervising teacher, makes some use of this space, sending students to work there during writing workshop and placing desks between the lab tables for those students who find it difficult to concentrate or stay out of trouble. The majority of the desks, used by the students during the large-group lessons which comprise most of the language arts period, are crowded together in one part of the room. Adding to the clutter are jackets hanging on the backs of chairs and backpacks on the floor near or under desks. The walls hold many charts, posters, and bulletin boards of student work, arranged rather haphazardly. Sitting on the lab tables are science materials used during the afternoon.

THE STUDENT TEACHER

Courtney Littleton, a longtime resident of Charter Hills, attended Grove School herself when it was a middle school. She graduated from the local university with a major in economics and worked for a time in the suburbs of a large city. She had always enjoyed baby-sitting, working with children in Sunday school, and giving music lessons. After two or three years she "just decided to face the truth that I wanted to be a teacher." Returning to her hometown, she began a master's degree and teaching certification program in elementary education, which she was completing during the time we observed her. Ms. Littleton is now teaching kindergarten in an adjoining county.

She told us that she wanted to be a teacher because she wanted to feel that she was doing some good for somebody. She believed her rapport with young children was a gift she should not waste. She had been a good student herself and had positive memories of her own life in school and particularly of her experience at Grove School 15 years earlier.

Ms. Littleton's internship at Grove School is her second school placement, having spent the first half of the semester in a kindergarten classroom at another school. She feels somewhat apprehensive about this second placement. She knows that "this particular group of kids had been 'failures' for several years." She is concerned that it might be difficult to excite them about learning.

She also finds that the system of discipline at the school, as codified in a "thick handbook," is in conflict with ideas from her education classes about using "a more cooperative approach, giving kids responsibility." She continues to struggle with decisions about the best approach, unsure of her own "philosophy on discipline." In our interviews, too, there are several occasions when she expresses doubts about her handling of a situation, finding a conflict between two principles of teaching and not knowing how to resolve it. Doubt is not reflected in her manner with the students, however; with them she nearly always seems calm and self-assured.

Perhaps Ms. Littleton's greatest concern in approaching her internship is her fear that she will get into a situation in which a "student says, 'No, I won't do it,' and, in front of the class." She had been intimidated by "kids like that" when she was at Grove School, and she fears she would be intimidated by them again. She tells us, however, that she has decided that if she reminds the student of the consequences of an action, it will be up to the student to decide whether to take the consequences or not. She has found that this attitude works well for her in the classroom.

As a student teacher, Ms. Littleton has some freedom in her planning, but she has to keep to the general outlines of what is planned for the class by the supervising teacher. She finds that the language arts period of 90 minutes is usually divided into three main parts. First, the students work on their spelling or vocabulary lesson, with an expected lesson for each day of the week. Then, working as a group, they nearly always read aloud and discuss the novel (paperback trade book) they are studying. The supervising teacher tells us that she herself began the year with two reading groups, but she found that with this class, whole-group instruction is more successful. Sometimes the students have a worksheet or brief written assignment during this portion of the period. They work independently on these while the teacher circulates to help them.

The final part of the language arts period is a writing workshop, which usually begins with a brief lesson for the whole group and continues with students working independently or conferencing with a friend on their writing assignments. Occasionally students form small groups to work on a specific project during either the second or the last part of the period, but at these times they are always allowed to form their own groups and work with their friends. Grouping by ability or achievement within the class is not used.

Ms. Littleton, aware that some of the students in the class are functioning at very low levels in reading and writing, is concerned that the prevailing arrangements in the class do not allow them to receive much of the individual attention she feels they need.

> I know who those students are, and I make a point of going around and checking on them, making sure that they at least understand what we are doing, helping them out. But as you see, I give them one minute at a time, and that's all I can do. I wish I could have given them more.

She also feels that the plan for language arts, which has the students reading only a series of children's novels during the course of the year, is too limited. She would like them to read other kinds of literature, but again her choice is restricted by her status as a student teacher.

Ms. Littleton's presentation of herself is quite distinctive. A tall, slim young woman with ash blond hair, she dresses in simple yet elegant clothes, often in gray, black, and white. Her physical appearance seems in keeping with her manner, which is usually subdued and calm. She speaks to the class in quiet and businesslike tones, telling them with a minimum of words what they need to know and what she wants them to do. The children seem to respond well to this style, which contrasts with the more voluble and dramatic self-presentation of their usual teacher. Ms. Littleton's gestures, too, are very controlled. She keeps her hands close to her body and makes small movements.

Ms. Littleton has a considerable rapport with the children. She has a sharp sense of humor, and frequently uses it to make a point gently or to defuse a potentially difficult situation. She also notices when a child falls behind in writing the spelling test, for example, or appears confused by the directions for a worksheet, and she moves quickly to make sure the problem is cleared up.

THE STUDENTS

When Ms. Littleton starts her student teaching at Grove, Ms. Arden's class is entering the last months of a year that their teacher has found very difficult. There are 20 children in the class—13 boys and 7 girls. Twelve children are Caucasian, 7 children are African-American, and 1 boy is Asian-American. Two of the boys in the class are classified as learning-disabled, and both are receiving resource help at other times in the day. One boy, Abel, is in the process of being assessed because his teachers believe he has a learning disability. He is the child we choose to focus on. We choose Abel because the two boys already receiving services are among the highest-achieving and best-behaved students in the class, while Abel is obviously having problems both academically and behaviorally. During the time of our observations, Abel begins receiving resource help, pending the completion of his assessment.

Somewhat to our surprise, given the description of the class provided by Ms. Arden, misbehavior is not a major problem in the class while we are there. Particularly during large-group activities and structured individual assignments, most children appear to be on task most of the time. Only twice do we see a student refuse to comply with a teacher's instructions, and both these confrontations are brief and mild. Most children seem to enjoy the novels they are reading. The few who do not display enthusiasm appear uninvolved, not actively resistant.

During some of the writing workshops, when students are supposed to be working independently on their own projects, there is considerable off-task activity. We notice that noisy and off-task behavior seems to come in cycles. A peak is reached, and a few moments later everyone can be observed working and concentrating. Then conversation rises again. From time to time Ms. Arden and Courtney reprimand the students as a group. But there are days when everyone seems to be working most of the time, and many of the students appear to be pleased and proud of their work. This is particularly true when the students are working on their "Modern Fairy Tales," a project in which they write up-to-date versions of traditional tales. These are carefully copied into bound books to be displayed at an open house for parents.

Abel stands out from the group in a number of ways. He is among the taller students in the room, only a few inches shorter than Ms. Littleton. His skin, hair, and eyes are all very light in color. He dresses in jeans, t-shirt, and sneakers, with a heavy leather or vinyl jacket on the colder days. His hair is cut short, and frequently he comes to school with the top of it sticking straight up, held in place with styling mousse. One of his ears is pierced and he often wears two earrings, one of which dangles two inches.

Abel's behavior is usually calm, but he frequently seems tuned out from what the class is doing. He spends time making paper airplanes, sharpening his pencil by rubbing it against the edge of his desk, or just looking around the room. If he is looking at the book during reading time, he tends to rest his head on the desk and look sideways at the page. He rarely raises his hand to respond to a question and, on the whole, seems to do as little work as possible. If the chalkboard contains a list of homework not turned in, his name is sure to be on it.

Still, when we conduct a stimulated recall interview with him, it is clear that he was alert to everything that goes on in the room. He has good insights into why things happen as well. Shown a videotape on which he appears to be doing anything but paying attention, he is able to describe the words and actions of students who are not shown in the picture and to interpret Ms. Littleton's actions as she had intended.

A TYPICAL LESSON IN MS. LITTLETON'S CLASS

It is a Wednesday morning, and by 8:15 most of the students in Ms. Arden's room are in their seats. Sean is turned around in his seat talking to Hugh, who sits behind him. Andrew and Adam are deeply wrapped up in a discussion of the horror movie they saw at a local theater on Sunday. Some of the other students are also chattering, but Donny, James, and Kim are sitting silently in their seats. Ms. Arden and Ms. Littleton are conferring at Ms. Arden's desk in the back of the room. The voice of the PA system is heard in the room, telling students and teachers which buses are late and which clubs will meet during the after-school activity period the next day. The voice ends by telling everyone to have a good day, and as it dies away Ms. Littleton moves to the front of the room and stands next to the first science table, slightly to one side of the center of the room.

"Please get out your paper for the practice spelling test. You should already have numbered your papers one to twenty." She waits while students retrieve spelling papers from desks and notebooks. "Andrew, this is not a time to talk." Ms. Littleton walks down the center aisle, leaning over to speak to one or two students whose papers are not ready. Returning to the front of the room, she says, "All right, put up your barriers." Those students who have not already done so put up a large dictionary so it stands between them and the student in the next desk. She walks over and adjusts the "barrier" between Hugh and Charles. The two boys are friends, and each usually sits in a desk isolated from the rest of the students. As an experiment, Ms. Littleton is letting them sit together this morning, and she is aware of a potential for problems.

"I am ready to begin," she says, using a very calm, firm tone of voice. The students respond instantly and sit silently, pencils ready. "Okay, the first word is '*relax*.' After school I like to relax." Every student is quiet, focused on writing the spelling word. This is a time when everyone is very clear on what he is supposed to be doing and does it without question. They move smoothly through the list. Ms. Littleton is watching to make sure she is not going too fast for them to keep up and to see which students may be missing a word that they would like her to repeat. Once, Abel asks her to repeat a word, but she tells him to wait until the end.

Soon they have reached the twentieth word. "Are there any words you want me to repeat?" Three hands go up. "Those of you who have all the words, go back and check your spelling and your handwriting."

Towanda asks, "What is Number seventeen?"

Ms. Littleton repeats the word. She responds to the other two students who have raised their hands, and then says, "Abel? Did you need a word?" Though he has not raised his hand, he asks for number six.

Because this is a practice test, they will check their own papers. Ms. Littleton reminds them to make a list of the words they missed "so you can be responsible for studying only the ones you need to." She says, "Let's go through these quickly." She calls on students to spell the words. Most of them spell correctly, especially since she makes a point of assigning the easiest words to the less able students. She repeats each correct spelling in a clear voice so all can hear.

Hugh misspells his word, and she prompts him. "You only left out one letter. Say it again. You know it." Now he spells the word correctly. She repeats his spelling and goes on. Ms. Littleton walks over to Abel and asks him if he is writing down the words he needs to study.

> He wasn't doing it. I reminded him to, but I didn't push it. It would just have been a big struggle, and we didn't need to take time to do that.

Ms. Littleton says, "This list was not too difficult. How many students already have one hundred on it?" About half the hands go up. "Good. Okay, put the paper in the spelling section of your notebook, and don't forget to study the words you missed for the test on Friday. Kathy, will you hand out these worksheets?" While Kathy starts to hand out the worksheets, Ms. Littleton goes over to where Hugh and Charles are sitting and speaks quietly to them, reminding them that letting them sit together at reading is a trial. Abel gets up and goes to the pencil sharpener. He sharpens, empties the sharpener, sharpens some more. He takes a long time to return to his seat.

The next activity is one that Ms. Littleton has brought to the classroom and has repeated two or three times during her stay there. On the worksheet is a list of vocabulary words taken from the novel the students are reading. Each word is given in the sentence in which it appears in the book. The students are to guess the meaning of the word from its context, write down their guess, then look up the word in the dictionary, copy its meaning, and compare their guess with the dictionary definition. The object of the activity, as Ms. Littleton explains to the students, is to help give them confidence in their own ability to determine the meaning of a word from the context in a book they are reading so that they will not give up when they find unfamiliar words.

Ms. Littleton's plan is to go over a few of the words as a group and then to give the students time to work independently on the rest of the list. She begins to talk, then stops, and waits a few seconds until everyone is quiet and begins again. She thinks:

> It's no point in giving directions if they're not all listening.

When she has reviewed the directions with the students, she reads the first sentence on the list: "'Their friendship was sealed together by a

mutual loss.' What do you think 'mutual' might mean?" Peter raises his
hand, is called on, and gives a definition. Ms. Littleton calls on several
others who add guesses similar to Peter's. Some of the students seem
really involved in this activity. It is clear they view it as a kind of game
in which they are trying to outguess the dictionary.

Ms. Littleton calls on Charles, who has looked up the word in the
dictionary. The definition he reads is very close to the ones they have
been giving. On the second word, Kamani, who is sitting in the back of
the room, has his dictionary in his lap and looks up the word without
being seen by Ms. Littleton. He raises his hand, is called on, and gives
his definition. "Very good, Kamani." When they have finished the first
two words, she tells the students they have 10 minutes to work on the
assignment. Everyone settles right down to work. Ms. Littleton
circulates around the room, stopping first at Kim's desk, though she has
not asked for help. She reasons:

> I wanted to make sure I helped Kim. She has a lot of trouble.

Next she helps Kathy, who has her hand up, and then walks over to
Bobbie, one of the weaker students in the class. They smile very
sweetly at one another.

> There are certain ones that I always need to check on, just to make
> sure they understand what's going on.

Charles raises his hand and calls softly, "Miss Littleton." She goes over
to help him.

Now she goes over to Abel and finds that he does not have a
worksheet. She gets him one, and he gets started. After a few moments,
she tells the students to put the worksheets away in their notebooks.
"You can work on them between eleven forty-five and twelve after
lunch, so you won't need to have them as homework. Now get out your
Cybil War [the novel they are reading]." The students put away the
worksheets and quietly get out their books. Some of them quietly move
into vacant desks near the front of the room or carry their chairs up to
fill in the center aisle. They have been doing this for the past few weeks
so that everyone can hear better during the oral reading.

When all the students are in their places and quiet, Ms. Littleton
says, "Yesterday with our partners we read 'An Hour of Misfortune.'
What was that about, for the people who weren't here yesterday?"

Hugh raises his hand to answer and gives a good summary of the chapter, which ends with the main characters making plans for a movie date. "What do you think is going to happen on this date?" Later she recalls,

> I asked this question to give them a purpose for their reading. That will help their comprehension.

Many of the students have ideas. She records them on the chalkboard, although she does not write down the silliest ones. There is a lot of enthusiasm. When the noise gets too loud, she shushes them, not crossly, but just to keep the noise down so they can continue. When the chalkboard is full, Ms. Littleton begins to read at the beginning of the chapter. She thinks,

> I want to get the reading off to a good start and to settle them down, too.

Hugh says something, and she stares at him while continuing to read.

Finishing a paragraph, she calls on Kathy to read. While Kathy is reading, Ms. Littleton walks down the center aisle, looking at the students' books. She stops and shows Andrew the correct page to be on. She likes to make sure people are not reading magazines under their desks, or are not six chapters ahead. She says, "Thank you, Kathy," and turns to Charles.

"Will you read, Charles?" He takes a minute to find his place.

> I see he is not paying attention, and I want him to be with us.

Charles reads with some hesitation. While he is reading, Ms. Littleton walks to the back of the room. Without a word, and without even catching Kamani's eye, she removes from his hands an origami crane he is playing with

> Oh, I'm just taking away Kamani's origami. You notice I don't bother anything about it. I usually just pick it up.

When Charles finishes a paragraph, she says, "Thank you, Charles."

Charles goes right on reading. Towanda, who is sitting behind him, hisses, "She said you could stop." Charles stops at the end of a sentence.

Ms. Littleton calls on Kim for a reading turn. Kim reads with great difficulty, stumbling on many of the words. When she reads *"taking"* for *"talking,"* Towanda says quietly, *"Talking."* Kim corrects herself and goes on. A few sentences later, Andrew helps her in the same way.

When Kim finishes, Ms. Littleton says, "Thank you, Kim. Matt, will you read?" Matt reads with some expression. No one helps him when he stumbles.

Ms. Littleton calls on Sally next, and after her turn they stop to discuss what is going on in the book. At the end of this brief discussion, in which children have joined without raising their hands, several children are calling out. She says, "Kathy has her hand up," but Kathy says she only wanted a turn to read. After one or two more comments, she calls on Kathy for a reading turn, and Kathy begins to read.

Towanda, who gets the next turn, pauses, struggling with the word *"pessimistically."* Ms. Littleton asks the class what the word means. No one seems to know, and she supplies the definition. Towanda goes on with her turn. Most of the students seem to be on task, but Peter stretches hard and starts playing with his hair. Ms. Littleton says, "Thank you, Towanda," and adds, "Let's stop for a minute and ask what did Simon find out on this infuriating date that was very surprising." She reasons:

> I find this part of the plot very confusing, so I figure they probably
> don't understand it either. It's so complicated. It's like a soap opera.

Andrew gives a long and basically correct response to the question, clarifying who said what to whom and why. Ms. Littleton adds some comments about his response. Charles and Hugh are talking to each other. Ms. Littleton asks who would like to read next, and Andrew comments softly, "I would never act like that."

Abel gets up and packs his backpack. He is going for his first session with the learning disabilities resource teacher. Ms. Arden goes over to him and helps him get his things together. They leave the room. No one seems to pay attention or to see the activity as other than routine.

Two more students have reading turns. Adam turns around to talk to Andrew, and Ms. Littleton says softly, "A-a-adam." He turns forward, but a minute later he turns back to Andrew to finish his sentence. Ms. Littleton begins to read. Hugh is whispering to Charles, and she says, "Hugh." Hugh stops whispering.

The end of the book is approaching. All of the students seem to be absorbed in it, although Andrew and Bobbie are both twitching their legs under their desks. One of the students makes a comment while Ms. Littleton is reading, and she laughs and raises her eyebrows. She later gives this explanation for her action:

> I'd better read because we are running out of time for the lesson. I want to make it easier for the students to enjoy the ending of the book.

They reach the last words of the book. Most of the students appear to be on task. Matt, Hugh, Charles, and Kim are not looking at their books but are quiet and seem to be listening.

Ms. Littleton asks, "How would you rate that book on a scale of one to ten?" Many voices answer: "Ten." "Nine." "Eight point five." "Six."

She flips the light switch off. There is only one small window in the back of the room, and whenever she does this, the room seems inky black for a moment. It is precisely nine o'clock when she flips the switch back on and says, "Put away your chairs and get ready for a mini-lesson. This better not take you guys forever." They move back to their seats rather quickly.

"Good," Ms. Littleton says. "Most of you got back quickly." She tells the class that they have only three weeks left in this nine-week grading period. Near the end of the nine weeks, she tells them, they will each select one best piece completed during the grading period and be graded on that one. "That will be your grade for this nine weeks."

She tells the students that today they will begin by reviewing the steps of writing workshop, since they have been working on something else for a while. She asks, "What are the steps?" There is a poster on the wall listing them, but neither Ms. Littleton nor the students refer to it or look at it during the following discussion.

Towanda raises her hand, and Ms. Littleton calls on her. She says that the first step is to conference with someone about your idea for your piece. Ms. Littleton nods, and adds that next you write your first draft without worrying about spelling, handwriting, or neatness. "What's next?" she asks. Kathy raises her hand. She says that you conference with someone, and that person is supposed to tell you what else they want to know about your subject. Ms. Littleton expands on this idea. "Next you write your second draft, and then what do you do?" she asks.

James raises his hand and is called on. "You edit your draft."

Ms. Littleton nods. "Then what?"

Kamani calls out, "Then you make your final copy."

"Okay," she says. "Since so many of you will be starting new pieces today, let's share our ideas for our pieces. Who would like to be first?"

Ms. Littleton writes the students' ideas on the chalkboard as they call them out. Andrew raises his hand and says that he wants to write about drugs and gangs in Los Angeles. Many of the ideas are about crime, drugs, and horror movies. She is thinking,

I'm concerned about the heavy emphasis on these topics in their writing, but right now I'm accepting the ideas they put forward.

Students are calling out with some excitement and commenting on one another's ideas. Each time Ms. Littleton turns around to write an idea on the board, the noise level rises. All the talk, though, seems to be about the writing ideas.

Peter turns around and is looking at Andrew. Ms. Littleton says, "Peter, turn around and put your feet under your desk. It will help to keep you from talking."

Peter says, "I wasn't talking."

"I know," she says, "but it will help you not to talk anymore." Peter turns around.

Ms. Littleton is bothered more and more by the noise level. She says, "Shhhh!" several times, flips the lights off once, and finally asks loudly for quiet. Silence falls, and she says, "Okay, who needs to conference?" Towanda and Lisa raise their hands. "Okay, Towanda and Lisa, I'm going to put a time on your conference, so be efficient. You can have seven minutes."

Towanda and Lisa go to conference behind the file cabinet. Ms. Littleton asks, "Okay, who wants to go to No Man's Land?"(This is Ms. Arden's name for the spaces between the science tables.) Adam and Kathy raise their hands. "Okay," says Ms. Littleton. She restates the rules for being in No Man's Land: "But you have to stay there the whole period, and no talking to anyone. Everyone else should be writing." The room is very quiet.

Ms. Littleton goes over to Peter and tells him that if he wants to conference he should raise his hand and she will find him someone to conference with. The noise level begins to rise. Adam, who is in No Man's Land, is talking to Andrew, who is at his nearby desk. Hugh and Henry raise their hands; they want to conference. Ms. Littleton is talking to Sean. Matt goes over to the publishing center to put his finished piece in a binding.

Adam and Andrew are talking again, but no one seems to notice. Ms. Littleton sees that Charles is out of his seat and calls out, "Charles, Charles, in your seat." He sits down. She goes to the back of the room and talks quietly with Ms. Arden. Now Adam, Donny, and Kamani are talking. Hugh turns around to talk to Dorian and Susie, who have been writing together. Andrew goes over to Ms. Arden and asks her for the spelling of a word. Kathy, who was in No Man's Land, is now at the front of the room talking to Lisa.

Although few of the students work steadily through the period, all but Hugh have done some writing at some point in the period, and the room does not get noisy. At 9:45 the bell rings. They have five minutes to prepare to go to their next class, and they begin, fairly noisily, to get ready to leave. When the bell rings at 9:50, they leave the room, chatting loudly. Ms. Arden reminds them to put their chairs under their desks before they go. One or two go back to do this before the room is empty.

QUESTIONS FOR REFLECTION

- What do you see as some of the strengths of Courtney's teaching at this stage in her career? What ideas would you suggest to her to improve her teaching?
- What values do you think are guiding Courtney's choices as a teacher? Are they ones you would hold if you were teaching in her context? Why or why not?
- Do you think Courtney's choices of instructional approaches are effective for special education students who would be integrated into her classroom? Are there different actions she could follow to improve their educational opportunities?

OVERALL FINDINGS

We identified three categories of themes: (1) those frequently observed in Ms. Littleton and common to other teachers in the case studies in this volume, (2) those less frequent with respect to Ms. Littleton though common to her and the other teachers, and (3) those peculiar to Ms. Littleton.

The first category consists of four themes that are common to all the teachers studied and also occur frequently with Ms. Littleton.

Watching Students As They Work

This theme consists of actions, such as monitoring seatwork or calling on misbehaving students, which demonstrates to students that Ms. Littleton both is aware of what they are doing and is committed to keeping them on task and attentive. This theme is one of the most frequently occurring ones.

Event: At the beginning of reading time, Ms. Littleton looks around the room before asking Kathy to begin reading.

Thought: I was waiting for everybody to get their books open. That's why I was looking around.

Event: While repeating words for the spelling test, Ms. Littleton says to a misbehaving student, "Henry, did you get them all?"

Thought: Henry was not paying attention. I knew he had them all.

Giving Hints and Clarifying

Events associated with this theme are those in which Ms. Littleton seeks to clear up perceived student confusion or in which she tries to help a student reach the correct answer.

Event: Ms. Littleton tells a student struggling to pronounce a word, "Pronounce it just like the six words before it."

Thought: I didn't want to tell Kathy how to pronounce it. I wanted her to figure it out. So I gave her those clues.

Event: During reading time, Ms. Littleton stops the class and asks, "What is the big step forward that Simon [a character in the novel] just made? He's talking about that he's made a step forward and doesn't want to step back."

Thought: I didn't want to let that go by. I really didn't think anybody understood that, so I felt it was important to stop and clarify what the character was talking about there.

Event: After explaining a writing assignment, Ms. Littleton asks, "What's one thing I might want to include if I were writing a description of the woods?" She then writes down suggestions on the board.

Thought: I'm trying to tie together what they just did with highlighting information from the book, to writing about the woods . . . trying to help them do this assignment . . . It's also modeling that I wanted the description in complete sentences and something that was not copied straight out of the book. You can use the information from the book without copying it.

Showing Awareness of Students' Needs and Differences

This theme centers around Ms. Littleton's awareness that each student brings to class a unique set of needs, both educational and psychological. Although many of Ms. Littleton's interactions with students are motivated by this theme, her knowledge about her students seems at times vague and superficial. It is likely, however, that the brevity of the student teaching experience would make this a shortcoming common among student teachers.

Event: Ms. Littleton checks on certain students to make sure they understand a worksheet they are completing.

Thought: There are certain people I try to keep up with during seatwork . . . because a lot of times they don't understand, and they won't say if they don't understand. They either sit there with a blank paper, or in the case with someone like Lisa, they will start talking out or acting out, and it's just because they don't understand what to do.

Building Students' Self-Concepts

This theme, which also includes encouraging self-responsibility and mutual respect, characterizes a large number of the events we observed. Ms. Littleton repeatedly expresses her desire to help students feel self-confident and more responsible for their own actions.

Event: Ms. Littleton asks whether anyone else would like to read his work and then comments, "We have some good writers. I know there are some good ones."

Thought: I was trying to encourage more people to share, just have confidence in what they have written, and I knew there were some good ones because I had gone around and watched them writing the day before.

Event: Ms. Littleton describes an exercise where students will guess the definitions of words by reading them in context.

Thought: This is an exercise that they have done before in determining meaning of words from context; and, just like I told them, another purpose of the activity is to . . . give them confidence that it is something they can do.

The next six themes, comprising the second category of themes, occur less frequently with regard to Ms. Littleton's own practice though they, too, are common to all of the other teachers studied in the project.

Providing Step-by-Step Directions

This theme centers around Ms. Littleton's explaining in a logical, ordered sequence what the students are to do. She not only gives clear directions but also knows how to avoid overwhelming students with too many directions within a given period of time.

Event: Ms. Littleton explains how to divide pages for a book signature. "In doing your book signature, count up how many pages in your book you're going to write on. Say you have eight pages to write on. . . . Take your whole paper like this and divide it up into eighths . . . and see about how much you are going to need to put on each page . . . Make sure it is a good place to make a break, though, like at the end of a sentence or the end of a particular section."

Thought: I'm giving them an example of how they might decide how much text to put on each page. I think it's something new for them, figuring something like that out.

Summarizing And Reviewing

This theme represents Ms. Littleton's attempt either to bring an instructional period to a close or to highlight the main points of an instructional period. Among the techniques she uses are webbing, simulated diary entries, drama, and hypothesis testing.

Event: Ms. Littleton says, "Yesterday, with our partners, we read 'An Hour of Misfortune.' What was that about, for the people who weren't here yesterday?"

Thought: I'm reviewing what has happened up to now. Yesterday, they read on their own, and some of them didn't get quite as far as others—and I expected them to finish it for homework . . . I wasn't sure how far they all had gotten, so we needed to have a review.

Event: After a student finishes reading, Ms. Littleton turns to the list of predictions produced by students and written on the board, and says, "So one of our predictions came true."

Thought: Checking back . . . keeping our list of predictions in mind . . . When one of them is proven or disproved I refer back to that. I just want them to be more active thinkers when they're reading.

Offering Praise

There are patterns as to how Ms. Littleton uses praise. With few exceptions, she rarely praises students for routine or preset answers, such as on quizzes or worksheets. Thus in the more businesslike atmosphere of spelling time, her responses are monotone and perfunctory. She often simply repeats the students' answers. In contrast, during reading time and writing workshop she offers animated and genuine praise for students' spontaneous, creative productions. Also, whereas the teachers in the other case studies tied praise to a reason, Ms. Littleton rarely explains clearly to students why she is praising them.

Event: After a student comes up with a good definition, Ms. Littleton says, "That's really good, Peter. I'm going to write that down."

Thought:	I thought that that was unusual that he would have come up with that word *characteristic*, and I hadn't thought of it . . . It probably is the best synonym for that word. I just wanted to recognize that.
Event:	Ms. Littleton asks the class a question, and Henry answers. She says, "Henry, that's good."
Thought:	Henry gave that response, that he was vain, and I was glad. He seemed lately to be really uninterested and uninvolved.

Making Connections to the Students' World

This theme describes Ms. Littleton's endeavor to make the lessons relevant to the students, to meet them where they are. Such attempts often include concrete examples to clarify more abstract terms or ideas. Although this theme occasionally arises during spelling time, her questions during reading time indicate more concentrated efforts to use this technique.

Event:	To explain the word, "postage," Ms. Littleton says, "I wanted to mail two letters this morning but I didn't have enough postage."
Thought:	I didn't believe that they really weren't familiar with the word, and I felt that if they heard it in context that they would know it. And it actually did happen when I said that sentence. A lot of them said, "Oh yeah, I know what that word is."
Event:	Ms. Littleton asks students, "Have you guys ever had a friend who you've been friends with for a long time, and then you sort of started to wonder about that person?"
Thought:	I always try to tie into their experiences as much as I can. It helps them a lot with reading, and with this book . . . It's a really good book for that because they can relate to a lot of events and relationships in the book, and they love to tell stories about themselves, too. So it keeps them involved.

Encouraging Participation

This theme includes both general participation and the idea of fairness—giving all students an equal chance to participate. The examples here center on Ms. Littleton's expressed desire that as many students as possible be actively involved in all activities.

Event:	When Lisa struggles with reading a definition aloud, Ms. Littleton goes over and says, "Let's see if I can help you."
Thought:	I was just helping her read. Her reading skills are pretty weak; but she always volunteers, and I want to encourage that.
Event:	Ms. Littleton calls on Kim to give a definition.
Thought:	Her verbal skills are kind of weak, but every once in a while I make myself stop and think, "Who haven't I been calling on? Have I been calling on the same people?" And looking at this, I find that I did call on the same people very frequently. I know that I do that, so I have to stop and tell myself, "Call on the others," because I have to give them a chance.

Checking for Understanding

As the example below illustrates, early experience taught Ms. Littleton the necessity of using this strategy. Often connected to activities associated with the earlier theme of providing step-by-step directions, this theme is handled in various interesting ways. Ms. Littleton tends to look to the interested and basically attentive students, though, rather than to the slower or passive ones, for affirmation of understanding. She shows, however, some awareness of which students will need individual attention to correctly complete an assignment.

Event:	Ms. Littleton asks, "If the sentence is not complete, what do you do, Eric?"
Thought:	I'm quizzing them to repeat the directions back to me to make sure they have them, because I had some experiences the week before in giving them directions and assuming that they understood, and then setting them to work and . . . finding out nobody understood the directions.

The last category consists of five themes not found in the other case studies of this volume. They are salient to our observations of Ms. Littleton and seem to differentiate her from the experienced teachers.

Promoting Efficiency

This theme is very prevalent. Although there are several subcategories within this theme—such as concern for completing a lesson as planned, awareness of time constraints, and unobtrusive correction—all of them are characterized by Ms. Littleton's desire to complete the lesson as smoothly and efficiently as possible. At times she seems obsessed with time, even at the risk of sacrificing what we consider to be more significant concerns. Perhaps, however, this represents a belief shared by many student teachers: that the primary criteria for their evaluations will focus upon their ability to accomplish the goals they have set. The several examples below reveal how this one concern seems to affect her actions in a variety of ways.

Event: Ms. Littleton looks over at Sean, who has gotten out of his seat, but she does not intervene.

Thought: Most of the time I just ignore that. I don't think it would be productive to call attention to it every time he's up. He's always up throwing a piece of paper away or something. Every once in a while, I have a little talk with Sean. A lot of times it's not worth it to stop the whole class to talk to somebody about something like that.

Event: Ms. Littleton walks over to Abel's desk and asks him if he is getting the spelling words down.

Thought: I was checking to see whether Abel was writing down the words as we were going along, and he wasn't. I reminded him to, but I didn't push it . . . It would just have been a big struggle, and we didn't need to take the time to do that.

Prompting Future Orientation

This theme demonstrates Ms. Littleton's attempt to encourage students to think ahead or to develop skills that will have long-term consequences.

Event: Ms. Littleton asks students to pose questions about what
                  may happen in the book.

Thought: I'm trying to get them to establish a purpose for their
                  reading, things they might be interested in finding out,
                  things to think about when reading a book.

Event: Ms. Littleton explains that if the students make their *k*'s
                  look like *h*'s, she will count them wrong and then asks,
                  "There are four words like that, so if you miss them all,
                  what would your score be?"

Event: After discussing the need to be more careful on making
                  k's, Ms. Littleton says, "I just want us to spend about five
                  minutes practicing those four words because I don't want
                  you to get those words wrong."

Thought: I was just emphasizing that by their carelessness they
                  would just be hurting themselves .... What I was
                  emphasizing was just taking care and paying attention and
                  that it did matter.

Applying Theory—Including Problems Doing So

Not noticeable on film or from our observational notes, this theme
arises from our analysis of Ms. Littleton's thoughts in the stimulated
recalls. Although tied to various events, this theme represents her
struggle to accommodate two sometimes opposing ideas: what she feels
a good teacher should do and the reality of the classroom. Her thoughts
reveal her growing realization that theories and ideas will not always
work nicely and neatly in the classroom but would need to be adapted.
Some of the dilemmas facing her include how to call on everyone
during questions and answers, even though some students are less able;
how to give everyone an opportunity to read, although slow readers
frustrate the class; and how to affirm students' self-concepts even when
they offer questionable answers.

Thought: I didn't worry about calling on enough people during
                  reading because I know that the way some people read,
                  it's really frustrating for the rest of the class. And I
                  haven't really decided what I think I should do about
                  that—how to deal with giving those people a chance to
                  read but not turning everyone else off from the book.

Event: Ms. Littleton defends a student's work she has read aloud, in which the student had confused present-day events with flashbacks.

Thought: They were saying she had done the assignment incorrectly, which was true. Her comprehension of it wasn't very good; she included flashback events as events that had happened that day. But I felt that it was more important for her not to feel bad about what she had written. So I didn't tell the kids that they were right, that that was a legitimate criticism. I don't know if I should have done that or not, but she had been hesitant about reading it in the first place, and I didn't want to cut it down.

Event: Andrew expresses his opinion that a character is "a cheat," and Ms. Littleton writes this idea on the board.

Thought: I didn't understand what Andrew was talking about here. It didn't seem to relate at all to his character being "a cheat" . . . but I wanted this to be their ideas. And I really wondered, you know. . . how much I should change it before I wrote it up there or whether I should just write up there exactly what he said, even if it made no sense. I don't really know what to do about that.

Using Humor

Although Ms. Littleton jokes and laughs with students at various times, she has a special use of humor in connection with correction. Endeavoring to unobtrusively correct students or to lessen the sting of more direct correction, she often uses humor.

Event: When students dawdle during a transition, Ms. Littleton says, "Guys, I'm losing my patience!" She then adds, "You made my feet hurt standing here so long."

Event: When few students raise their hands when she asks for volunteers, Ms. Littleton says, "Oh great, a lot of volunteers today!" adding with a smile, "I want to see every hand up."

Cuing For Appropriate Behaviors

This final theme represents Ms. Littleton's effort to prevent anticipated misbehavior by providing students with appropriate alternatives. Although these actions are similar to those that characterize the theme of providing step-by-step directions, Ms. Littleton's thoughts indicate that they serve a different purpose.

Event: Ms. Littleton says, "When you are finished, put your pencils down so I'll know."

Thought: I usually say that just . . . as a cue to myself so I know when people are done. And another reason is just so they know something specific to do and won't just go off the wall.

Event: While repeating the spelling words, Ms. Littleton tells students, "If you got them all, look them over and check your handwriting and spelling."

Thought: I knew some of the ones that were sure that they had them all right were going to start fidgeting and doing other things. I wanted to give them a task. It's important for them to check their work.

CONCLUSION

Ms. Littleton is clearly an intelligent student teacher, dedicated and concerned about her students. She does many of the same things and has many of the same thoughts that, according to the other case studies in this book, are characteristic of teachers who are effective with classes that include mainstreamed special education students. How then is she different from those teachers? Do some of the differences she displays seem likely to be characteristics she shares not only with other student teachers but perhaps with experienced teachers who may be less effective?

Ms. Littleton is like the effective teachers in her careful attention to keeping students on task and her efforts to make learning easier by giving hints to students and trying to clear up their confusions. Like them, she tries to connect what is happening in the classroom to the real-world interests of her students, and she makes frequent efforts to encourage all students to participate in classroom activities and to see that every student has a turn at many of these activities.

On the other hand, she differs from them in significant ways. Effective teachers are acutely aware of individual students' needs and differences. Ms. Littleton shows such awareness less often and frequently on a superficial level. Rather than try to know precisely what an individual student needs and respond to that need, she frequently groups students in her mind. For example, she refers to "certain people I try to keep up with during seatwork."

Effective teachers use praise often and usually tell students just how they had earned praise. Ms. Littleton offers praise only during activities that she judges to involve student creativity or for truly outstanding accomplishment; most often she simply acknowledges the correctness of student responses. She rarely tells students why she was praising them, often saying simply, "That's good, very good."

Although Ms. Littleton works to improve the self-concepts of her students, her approach in this area differs from those of the other effective teachers in this volume. Each of them expresses the belief that students will learn best if they feel good about themselves. Therefore, they look for opportunities to enhance the children's self-image. Ms. Littleton's efforts along this line are somewhat different. She works to build students' self-concepts by encouraging them to accept responsibility for their own actions and to show respect for others in the classroom.

Effective teachers take many steps to be sure that students understand what they are supposed to do, what they are doing, or what they have done. Although Ms. Littleton sometimes gives step-by-step directions to students, this is not a frequent action and often occurs only when an exceptionally complex task is to be performed. She sometimes checks to see whether students have understood the directions for or the content of an activity, but often seems to confine this checking to the more able or more tuned-in students in the class.

Ms. Littleton also has some concerns that are not shared by the effective teachers in the other case studies, and these concerns seem to affect her actions significantly. She frequently worries about getting through the lesson on time, and on time means "to the minute." The major transition in the language arts period is between the reading portion of the time and the writing workshop portion, and it is scheduled to take place at nine o'lock. Ms. Littleton consistently makes that transition within two minutes of the scheduled time, and several times she has to rush the students in order to accomplish that. Although her decisions about how to handle undesirable student actions seem appropriate to us, they are often influenced by not wanting to spend time on such "off-task" matters. One of the teachers in this volume also is concerned about time pressures and often feels frustrated that it is not possible to spend more time teaching a given concept, but she apparently does not transform this frustration into pressure on the students or let it shape her classroom actions.

Also, Ms. Littleton gives considerable energy to encouraging the students to be oriented to the future. She is clearly far more concerned about grades than are the students. She pushes the students to think about what they are doing in terms of longer-term goals. We are unsure as to whether this was helpful to this particular group of students.

Ms. Littleton frequently shares her feeling of uncertainty about what is the most appropriate course of action in a given situation. She feels that she is faced with dilemmas which she has not yet learned how to resolve. Often these involve conflicts between principles that she holds about teaching and the realities of classroom experience. But she seems quite sure that she will be able to solve these problems in the future.

Some of Ms. Littleton's differences from the effective teachers in the other case studies seem to be directly related to her lack of experience and her brief tenure in the classroom. These might include her relatively superficial awareness of students' individual needs and differences and her concern about not knowing what to do in certain situations.

Another of the differences, though—her "future orientation" and concern with grades—might be associated with her own personality and experience. It is difficult to be sure whether it helps her to be effective with these students and whether it is appropriate for them.

Other differences, however, might be characteristics of less effective teachers. These could include her infrequent and nonspecific use of praise; her failure to be sure that all students—both the tuned-in and the tuned-out—are clear about what was being done or learned; and her concern with keeping to a preset schedule.

Further research involving experienced but less effective teachers would be helpful to determine which of Ms. Littleton's differences from effective teachers result simply from her extreme inexperience, which are personal, and which might be common contributors to teacher ineffectiveness in classes with mainstreamed special education students.

QUESTIONS FOR REFLECTION

- Which of the themes that describe Courtney's teaching are ones that you value? Why are they meaningful to you?

- Which of the themes do you think are important for facilitating the successful inclusion of students with learning disabilities into general education classrooms? How do they help meet the needs of special education students in such settings?

CHAPTER 8

Metaphor and Interpretation

Mary Catherine Ellwein
University of Virginia

The preceding case studies afforded glimpses into the world of teaching students with learning disabilities. Each of the five glimpses tells us "a way the world is" by revealing some of the thoughts and actions of a teacher (Goodman, 1982, p. 135). We first read of Marcia, a beginning teacher, and her practice during a reading lesson in a fourth-grade classroom. Juxtaposed to this account is a second case study recording a language lesson in Sue's third-grade classroom, a lesson informed by 20 years of practice. Following is a third case presenting the actions of Joyce, another teaching veteran, in a fifth-grade classroom where four of 24 students were mainstreamed students with disabilities. The next case study placed us in Anne's resource room, and finally the last case study returned us to a regular fifth-grade classroom to read of Courtney's experience as a student teacher. How can these case studies, these varied glimpses, inform practice and research on teaching in mainstreamed classrooms?

In this chapter, I shall attempt to explore these cases, commenting on certain metaphors expressed by the participating teachers and speculating upon a few metaphors suggested to me by my reading of the case studies. Metaphors "pervade everyday life, not just in language, but in thought and action" (Lakoff & Johnson, 1980, p. 3). They influence what we see and do not see in a particular situation as well as how we interpret that situation and choose to act within it. As Schön (1979) has argued, metaphors are both a way of making sense of reality and a means of gaining new perspectives of the world. By identifying the metaphors we use when we think and talk about teaching, we can examine both their utility and their restrictive capacity. Perhaps we may even enable ourselves to change behavior.

First, I will discuss how their own expressed metaphors influenced Sue and Joyce and served to organize much of what they knew about teaching and to determine what they chose to do in the classroom. Second, I will speculate upon certain images and metaphors which, to me, were latent in the representations of Marcia, Anne, and Courtney and of their practices. These images and metaphors in the second category were not articulated by the three teachers; however, they will permit me to comment on how metaphors influence researchers who write case studies and the readers of those case studies. I will, in addition, subject my own interpretation of one case study to analysis. Finally, I will conclude by discussing how metaphor can be a source for helping teachers reflect on practice and, perhaps, seen to generate new ways of thinking.

When teachers and researchers engage in studies like the ones reported in this book, they participate in the individual and joint construction of meaning. During interviews, teachers usually know more than they say and say more than researchers understand or see as relevant. Asked to reflect, teachers often construct new understandings of their work. Researchers, for their part, construct meanings and interpretations through the way they report and represent their data and their subjects. Inevitably, case studies are "stories" of a sort, since the authors are representing their understanding of what teachers say they know and do (Geertz, 1973). Clearly, the cases are not fictitious inventions of the authors, but constructed *representations*, created in part by (1) an exchange of ideas with teachers and (2) reference to the researchers' own knowledge and understandings about teaching.

Ultimately, the readers of case studies will construct interpretations of their own as they bring their own histories and knowledge to bear upon the text and create new understandings. This chapter is my own interpretation, fashioned from my own understandings and engagement with the text. Like you the reader, I had no direct contact with the teachers; my only way of knowing them was through the researchers and their cases.

TEACHERS' METAPHORS

A number of researchers have investigated metaphors and images held by teachers (Clandinin, 1985; Elbaz, 1983; Munby, 1986; Munby &

Russell, 1990; Provenzo, McCloskey, Kottkamp, & Cohn, 1989; Tobin, 1990). Some of these studies were founded on the notion that teachers' images are part and parcel of their practical knowledge. Elbaz (1983) defined practical knowledge as a "complex, practically-oriented set of understandings which [teachers] use actively to shape and direct [their] work" (p. 3). Further, Clandinin (1985) argued that practical knowledge is highly personal in that an individual's actions and circumstances "leaven" the textbook or theoretical content (principles, skills, procedures) of teaching (p. 362).

Practical knowledge can be discerned in how a teacher acts as well as in how she describes her work. Although Elbaz (1983) concluded that such knowledge could be expressed in forms such as rules (simple and automatic routines) and principles (reasoned guides to action), images were taken to be the most important to a teacher's style. Images are formed on the basis of a teacher's "feelings, values, needs and beliefs...and [she] marshals experience, theoretical knowledge, and school folklore to give substance to these images" (p. 134). Like metaphors, images serve to inspire a teacher, and they guide her in making sense of future teaching situations.

Although not designed to study teachers' metaphors or images, the cases of Sue and Joyce document metaphors that permit us to speculate about the images they appear to hold. By examining their metaphors, we can come to a better understanding of how their similar, even generic teaching rules and principles are "leavened" with their personal histories and experiences to produce very different classroom events.

Like many of the teachers studied, Sue evinced principles that included references to student involvement, building students' self-concepts, checking for understanding, linking and integrating lessons, and awareness of students' needs. However, Sue's image of herself as a teacher and her view of the learning process led to instructional events that differed from those in the other cases. At the time of the study, Sue's professional image was that of the writer, and she democratized this image by encouraging her students to see themselves in a similar manner.

Sue did not view the classroom as a place in which the teacher delivers knowledge to students; such an image was not consonant with the image of teacher as author. Instead, she viewed the classroom as a workshop where students and teachers were partners in the construction of understanding. Sue perceived education as "talking, sharing, and communicating." She wanted students to leave her workshop with a love of and excitement about learning. The image of a workshop resulted in distinct instructional organization: whole-group discussion, individual choice during independent writing, and small-group reading instruction. In the whole-group activity, she solicited and accepted ideas without requiring students to raise their hands before recognition to speak. Children chose writing partners, while Sue made sure that everybody was engaged before sitting down to do her own writing. She encouraged children to share their work in informal conversation with her and with other students and informal sessions like the "author's chair time." Sue wanted students to learn about tasks that were meaningful to them as writers. In the small reading group where they worked in concert, she would announce, "We're going to be editors," as she did to set the tone and purpose for the lesson on quotation marks. In these groups the more experienced "colleague" shared information with the neophyte and assisted learning by matter-of-factly correcting missteps as they occurred.

Like other teachers, Sue maintained that student involvement and participation was a valued principle, and she employed a number of rules which gave form to that principle. To realize her image of authors in a workshop setting, Sue diminished the overt focus on the teacher and underscored the role of the setting and social organization. Sue's talk was free of references to control and constant responsibility. In fact, Sue was convinced that easing her control over such things as determining what children would write allowed her students to produce better work and learn more. Her rejection of overt and constant control did not eliminate rules and structure, however. She imposed classroom rules that would allow activity to proceed free from her unrelenting monitoring. As evidenced during the writing time, students worked with little need of external discipline or redirection. Choices were available and negotiations common, for example, about the amount of time to be spent on an activity.

The democratized image of writers in a workshop setting, albeit one in which Sue had the greatest amount of expertise, influenced the way Sue spoke about children. Her comments were not filled with conclusions about students' level of motivation or interest. When she did speak of the special needs of children in the "low-level" groups, it was a specific comment on what they needed to learn to be successful. Sue maintained that students needed to be able to (1) use strategies and (2) make connections with knowledge already learned, but she was not the only one responsible for students' learning. According to Sue, students gain independence through learning strategies, sharing responsibility, and being alerted to priorities and expectations.

Consistent with the somewhat blurred distinctions between teacher and students, when Sue commended the efforts of her students, she spoke of her respect rather than her pride. She engaged in active listening to communicate her respect and to encourage an increased sense of self-worth. She believed that principles upholding individual esteem had value in the world beyond the writing workshop.

The case of Joyce revealed two images of teaching that she seemed to hold as important to her practice: she was at once a survivor and a manager. The former image was rooted in her personal life experiences, and she used it to inform her relationships and interactions with her students. As related in the case, Joyce came from a place and time as limited as that of many of her students; and as a result, she believed that she had empathy for them: "I've been there, too." Empathy was not enough for Joyce; she maintained that she had to have specific knowledge of her students' lives and times. This informed empathy was prerequisite to effective teaching.

Congruent with her image of surviving, Joyce maintained that education is learning how to live rather than the "amount of knowledge pouring in"; education is a process as opposed to a commodity. As a result, she claimed that feeling good about oneself and being able to work with other people were of greater import than digesting subject matter. Influenced alike by her image of education and her belief that many children have low self-esteem, Joyce affirmed the need to promote positive self-concepts. Like Marcia and Sue, she praised students for effort as well as for correct answers. Like Sue, she espoused the principle of active listening and noted its value during reading group time:

> It's one of the few times during the day where they get to really express themselves and where they get to be listened to carefully. I think they really thrive on feeling like what they have to say is important.

Joyce likened the demands of a classroom composed of "problem" students as a challenge to survival. One must be self-sufficient: "You just learn how to be a really skillful manager of time and materials and resources." Classroom rules and routines allowed for management of the most important resource: her students. Structure would enable teacher and students to survive both in and out of the classroom. Rules for acceptable and unacceptable behaviors were specific, clear, and public in the classroom. Other routines were manifested when children completed tasks or switched activities with no direction from Joyce. Because students had internalized these routines, Joyce could teach and students could learn unfettered by interruptions. On occasions when the classroom code needed external enforcement, Joyce, who organized reading instruction according to a traditional three-group model, frequently substituted nonverbal cues, a snap or pointed finger, for verbal reprimands, aware that the latter would serve as yet another distraction for the students. With nonverbal cues, she could redirect students working in other groups or those engaged in independent work without interrupting the flow of her current group instruction.

Joyce spoke of instruction in terms of survival. She offered strategies to help students "cope" with textual encounters. She urged them to "prove it by the text," a technique helpful to all students, and to "bump unknown words," a strategy for those having extreme difficulty decoding. Drawing pictures, she maintained, could make difficult concepts concrete and facilitate reading comprehension. When a student could not answer a question correctly, Joyce often invoked the "choose a helper" principle, apparently believing that survivors know how to seek helpers. Students, she seemed to think, were likely to assist one another effectively. She herself acted as a specialized "helper" who could offer reading strategies or distribute mechanical aids like a ruler to place beneath a line of text.

However, to encourage self-reliance, Joyce might delay her assistance, wait to "give clues," or stall before calling on a student who was ready to aid others in their deliberations. Joyce had specific ideas about children with learning disabilities; they suffered from a "tendency to quit" and to "look for clues from other people." Her survival metaphor became apparent as she discussed their needs relative to those characteristics: children with learning disabilities need individual attention, "opportunities to perform," "all the advantages they can get," and urging to "think for themselves."

The preceding cases provided evidence that the image of writer influenced Sue in her teaching practice and that the image of survivor and manager influenced Joyce in hers. Clearly, we should not presume that these images are the only or even the most influential, but they are so consistent with the teachers' own statements and with the researchers' observations that we can conclude they must be important to the teachers themselves. In addition, we can ponder their contribution to the distinct classroom procedures instituted by teachers who professed similar teaching principles.

Although the cases of Marcia, Anne, and Courtney suggest certain influential images, they do not provide adequate evidence to identify images that the teachers would claim as their own. Nevertheless, readers are bound to construct images of their own to account for the representations in the case studies, and speculation about sources of influence is an inescapable part of interpretation. What follows are my own speculations as a reader of the case studies; I do not claim that the images were held by the teachers themselves but only that these images are part of my interpretation of the case studies. With my position established, I feel free to dispense with burdensome qualifications such as "it seemed to me" or "as I read the case."

A distinct image emerged from the representation of Marcia and her instructional practice: she was central to and powerful in the lives of her students. The image was most apparent in her views on the teacher's role in learning and on the development of student self-concept. Marcia's own maxim best sums up her beliefs about the role of the teacher in student learning: "If you're not teaching, the students are not learning." For Marcia, learning and instruction were directly and inextricably bound; the former did not occur in the absence of the latter. Several of her instructional principles evoke this image of a central and powerful teacher. Marcia, who believed that she could not teach without the full and undivided attention of the students, used the "focus" clue to gain it. Once she had ready students, she generally adhered to a recitation model of questions and answers, believing that students' answers provided the basis for and evidence of learning. So that Marcia could know what students knew, everyone was subject to responding to questions: "No one is off the hook." She used various techniques during her questioning, including "wait time" and "polling for agreement." Marcia saw wait time as an important technique in light of beliefs about her students:

> This group [of students] is so low that wait time is really important
> . . . . It takes some students a long time to get the answer right. . . .
> They'll have to sit there and think and think and then they'll raise
> their hand.

When Marcia "polled for agreement" to check students' understanding, she was mindful of her influence on students' so she tried to remain neutral while surveying students to prevent them from looking to her for the answer.

Questioning, she believed, also served to promote student involvement, a necessary condition for learning. According to Marcia, if a student showed evidence of straying, a question would serve the same purpose as "focus." Acting, another multipurpose strategy, made things real or concrete for those who had not caught on by questioning; but it also kept all entertained and therefore involved or focused. Marcia also believed she could maintain involvement by encouraging answers and praising risk taking as well as correct answers.

At the close of the lesson, Marcia spoke of "giving" students closure by reviewing to reinforce learning and to identify misunderstandings. Her choice of words reveals an image of a teacher who delivers a commodity, that of knowledge and understanding. Indeed, many of her statements represent knowledge as a commodity, including her reference to discovering "*how much*" a student knew.

Marcia's principles for the organization of instruction were in line with her maxim "If you're not teaching. . . . " She believed that whole-group instruction with minimal amounts of independent seatwork maximized learning time for her students. Her own statement reveals her emotional commitment to providing instruction:

> It makes me angry to go by teachers' rooms and see the kids doing independent work first thing in the morning; that's the very time [students] are freshest.

The case represents a teacher concerned with power and control. Marcia said it was essential for students to think she had control and authority; control was justified by her view of students as reluctant learners. She coaxed ("It's easy") or tricked ("It's hard") them into learning or, at least, participating. She had to "get through" to students; she spoke as if students were behind *barriers* which she had to remove before they could learn. She saw her students as neglected, overchallenged by prior teachers, and reluctant to learn because of past failures. Consequently, Marcia, who felt she should strive to "make students feel good about themselves," saw herself as figuring prominently in the achievement of this goal. Her statements not only assert her responsibility and desire to enhance the students' esteem but also imply her *power* to do so. She believed that praising students for trying, answering correctly, and near misses not only kept their attention focused but also stimulated development of positive self-worth. She also assumed that her pride in students and their efforts would be a positive influence in the development of healthy self-concepts.

The case of Anne represents the work of a special education teacher in a resource room populated by students of varying grade levels and exceptionalities. With its emphasis on Anne's choice and use of an instructional approach, the case presents the image of the teacher as a supervisor whose work is technical and externally driven. The source of this image is Anne's appeals to the principles of direct instruction which she used to meet her primary objective: to teach students skills and strategies that they lacked. Direct instruction, which she described as "fast-paced," allowed her to maintain student involvement by soliciting a "high percentage of responses from all of the children." Anne's actions during the whole- and small-group lessons were as structured and routine as those of her students. Several rules guided her interactions with students in the vowel teams lesson. By her announcement to "get ready," she cued students to recite. She used hand signals to direct students' attention to the words or letters on the board and to regulate their responses. At the conclusion of the activity and before the start of the next, she assigned points to students on the basis of their participation and promptness of responses.

She varied this general model slightly during the small-group reading lessons. The instructional materials, packaged as "corrective reading," provided Anne with a script for her lessons which prescribed the general procedures she followed, specific questions she asked, and the assignments she gave during the small-group lessons. The episode began when students read in unison, first individual words and then sentences at a pace set by Anne. Having cued students to wait, she asked questions in the manual and signaled them to respond in unison. When an answer did not match that specified in the manual, she supplied the correct answer and asked the student(s) to repeat it verbatim. Quickly, during transition to the next activity, Anne delivered tokens and assigned points for the activity just completed.

This instructional practice imposed an image of the classroom as a workplace where students as workers and the teacher as supervisor operated with clearly defined routines. Students worked to earn external rewards such as points; they could "spend" their hard-earned currency for a reprieve from work on Fridays—for fun. Anne had a direct role in monitoring and regulating their work, but this role, too, was dictated by an operator's manual composed by a group of expert engineers who had defined teaching as a set of techniques and routines. Deviations from the routine, such as not keeping up with the pace of the group or providing answers that did not match the standard, warranted Anne's quick and predictable attention. Situations not covered in the manual—students' questions, for example—provoked anxiety and uncertainty about how to respond. The instructional practice created its own "teacher-proof" image; Anne's adherence to this practice left little room for a competing image of her own.

Although other teachers valued the principle of teaching students skills and strategies that they lacked, none but Anne elevated it to the primary objective. In fact, Anne conceived of knowledge as skills and strategies. She believed that such knowledge had to be broken down into constituent parts or a sequence of steps, taught directly and internalized via recitation. The word *learning* was conspicuously absent from Anne's statements. Instead, students were said to "do" centers, "work," "get ready," "respond on cue," "receive points," "answer questions," "wait," "repeat corrections," "perform," "show," "move their mouths," "be heard," "talk up," and "read in unison or alone."

In Anne's classroom, the form of instruction dictated the rules; content and participation could vary only slightly. As a result, students placed in a special classroom on the basis of their exceptionalities were taught in a uniform manner.

The final case study represented a student teacher's efforts both to teach and learn in a fifth-grade class composed of "low-achieving students" and integrated students with learning disabilities. Courtney, the teacher, did not articulate metaphors that guided her actions, nor did the case study, as written, reveal any clearly dominant image. Russell, Munby, Spafford, and Johnston (1988) have observed that, although metaphors serve as guides to practice for experienced teachers, they are not so powerful for less experienced teachers. For these teachers, metaphors "seem to function more as indications of [their] level of experience and professional knowledge" (p. 39). The case showed Courtney to be both confident and uncertain as she made sense of her experience and situation in her cooperating teacher's classroom, and a plausible image would designate her a "confident struggler."

With confidence, she discussed her developing practical knowledge about instruction, espousing principles similar to those advocated by the more experienced teachers; she spoke of monitoring students' work, calling on students to maintain their involvement, and checking for understanding. However, Courtney's statements of principle, unlike those of the experienced teachers, resembled textbook descriptions in their detachment from a specific context. For example, she posed a question "to give them a purpose for their reading. That will help their comprehension." Although an important principle, it had no apparent or specific connections to her students or the lesson in question. Other descriptions were more contextualized, but they revealed an excessive reliance on her own reactions. For example, she posed another question because

> I didn't want to let that go by. I really didn't think anybody understood that there. So I felt it was important to stop and clarify what the character was talking about.

Or another instance:

> I found this part of the plot very confusing, so I figured they probably didn't [understand] either.

In both instances, she assumed that her students would react as she had done.

Courtney believed that low-functioning students needed more individual attention but did not specify what that meant. When it came to attending to students, she could cite that someone "has a lot of trouble" or that there are "certain ones that I always need to check on, just to make sure they understand what's going on." The statements imply some awareness of an individual student's needs but carry little specification. Contrast these statements with Joyce's reason for checking on Billy's comprehension:

> Billy has a problem with short-term and long-term memory. He can decode the words, but he has no comprehension. So I want to, very quickly, right as he's finishing his reading, to get him to zero back in on what he has learned from it.

Courtney struggled with the whole-group reading instruction and believed that it was not conducive to meeting the needs of her students. Her statement, "I wish I could have given them more," speaks of a thwarted sense of achievement as well as evokes the image of a teacher who delivers a commodity—in this instance, assistance and attention. We do not know how she would organize instruction if not constrained by the cooperating teachers' practices.

Frequently she encountered and created conflicts. For example, she worried about calling on everyone to read versus only calling on those who could read. She could not resolve the conflict between two values: providing equal opportunity versus minimizing frustration. She did not examine the routine of round-robin reading as a source of conflict and something amenable to change. Another apparent conflict made her feel that she could not enhance students' self-concepts while providing instructional correction. She was unable to restate her principles to accommodate both. She sent conflicting messages to students. For example, she would ask for volunteers, and in the same breath demand unanimous response—a show of hands from everyone. When managing the classroom, she wanted students to accept responsibility for their actions, but she seemed reluctant to specify consequences students would face. Courtney was ambivalent about rules, as she saw them in conflict with a "more cooperative approach giving kids responsibility."

METAPHORS AS WAYS TO ACCOUNT FOR DIVERSITY

Recent research tells us that teachers' knowledge and actions cannot be adequately or authentically represented in terms of teaching rules and principles that transcend space and time (Clandinin, 1985; Connelly & Clandinin, 1985; Elbaz, 1983). Of course, teachers' actions (knowledge-in-use) can be distilled to lists of routines, skills, and axioms. But what we lose in the distilling process may be the very essence of what we want to understand: how teachers assimilate and accommodate accepted principles in the context of their personal histories, their aspirations, and their particular classroom situations. In short, teaching is more than a set of rules and principles. We need to know *how* principles are interpreted and put into practice.

Attention to teachers' metaphors and images may very well help us understand and express more fully what it means to teach. Clandinin (1985) maintains that "verbal and practical images need not be clearly articulated and logically definable in order to exert a powerful influence in teachers' lives" (p. 383). Although the teachers in our case studies were not asked to identify their images or confirm the ones discussed in this chapter, the cases present observational and verbal evidence that permit us to examine metaphors and to speculate about images in an effort to come closer to understanding how generic principles can produce a range of classroom events and very different teachers.

MINDING OUR METAPHORS

Metaphors made public are metaphors that can be "minded." Since metaphors and images exert their influence on both the authors and the readers of case studies, those who write about teaching need to acknowledge the metaphors and images that they present to readers. Although representations like our case studies are unavoidably partial and value-laden views of teachers and teaching, alert readers are better prepared to interpret and evaluate case studies—and even to reject representations that seem unduly predetermined.

When I chose the metaphor to describe Anne, I was aware that my choice implied evaluation and determined emphasis. By selecting teacher knowledge in use as supervisor, I would inevitably emphasize certain elements in the case study and ignore others. For example, I would refer to the scripted actions and interactions with children, the regulated pacing, the reading in unison, the search for textbook answers, and the distribution of tokens as supporting evidence of the metaphor. Of course, not everything detailed in the case supported my metaphor, and so I dismissed certain elements, including the account of why she became a teacher, her specific knowledge of children, her manner of learning new teaching methods, and the constraints of the setting. I hesitated to use teacher-as-supervisor because it carried what many—myself included—would consider negative connotations. Therefore, I searched for and experimented with other, more neutral metaphors. The best of the alternatives seemed to be teacher as cook, one who conscientiously follows recipes word for word. Although Anne's reliance on the teacher's manual, her precise measuring of student responses, her belief in knowledge ingredients (skills) were consistent with this metaphor, it failed to account for several elements that were emphasized in the original study, particularly for students' activities and interactions.

In our increased preoccupation with metaphor and image, we need more than mere awareness, although a list of metaphors in current use is certainly interesting, in and of itself, including as it does characterizations of teacher as executive (Berliner, 1990); supervisor of complex technology (Cohen & Lotan, 1990); facilitator (Tobin, 1990);

mother, traffic cop, preacher, and trainer. Minding our metaphors is more than acknowledgment; it entails deliberation and dialogue. Writers who follow the lead of Goodman and Elgin (1988) should explore the "rightness" of each metaphor, its usefulness, its denotative and connotative contributions to any representation. Connelly and Clandinin (1988) have argued that it matters whether

> we think of teaching as gardening, coaching, or cooking. It makes a difference if we think of children as clay to be molded or as players on a team or as travelers on a journey. (p. 71)

And it makes a difference whether we see teachers as authors, survivors, or supervisors.

At the outset of this chapter, I expressed my belief that an examination of overt and latent metaphors can assist teachers in the search for better self-understanding. Whether conscious knowledge would also enable them to change practice is more problematic, although such an outcome is obviously attractive to teaching supervisors. In his optimistic work, Tobin (1990) characterizes metaphor as a "master switch" to change teacher beliefs and associated action:

> Teachers can identify the salient metaphors for specific teaching roles and consider whether or not alternatives would lead to improvements in the classroom. If teachers decide to alter the metaphors they use to understand particular roles, beliefs previously associated with the role might be perceived to be no longer relevant to that role. Beliefs consistent with the new metaphor can then be deemed relevant and influence what teachers do as they plan and implement the curriculum. (p. 126)

From a position of such optimism, one could imagine, for example, Marcia from our case studies attempting, with assistance from an interested colleague (or even on her own), to explore the implications of the teacher-as-leader image (assuming that this image was indeed one of several that she held about her practice). Any interested supervisor would certainly want her to examine the extent to which some of her beliefs and practices, such as whole-group recitation, teacher-directed instruction, and students as reluctant learners, were congruent or incongruent with the teamwork image noted in Chapter 3, one which Marcia had overtly endorsed. To the extent that her practices were not congruent, she would then have the opportunity to consider new metaphors or practices that could better accommodate her professed concern for teamwork: cooperative learning, teacher as coach, and students as eager players. Perhaps Marcia would begin to see that her assumption of total responsibility and her consequent frustration with inadequate time had forced her to resort to single practices to serve multiple purposes. Perhaps, she who had expressed appreciation of "no one looking over [my] shoulder, monitoring every move" would even come to see the irony of placing students in the very situation she detested.

Despite the optimism generated by current interest in metaphor as a source for change, we must not forget that metaphor is not a teacher's only reality. So long as extant teaching situations isolate teachers and deprive them of time for reflection and dialogue, the mere identification of metaphors and images will do little to help them alter current strategies used to get the job done. Any supervisory interventions that promote the exploration of metaphor must be carefully considered and scheduled. Without provision for dialogue and discussion, teachers who are unable to envision new images or reorganize their current repertoire of strategies will receive no assistance.

CHAPTER 9

Students' Perceptions of Teachers and Teaching

Deborah J. Gallagher
University of Northern Iowa

Melody J. Tankersley
Kent State University

Joanne M. Herbert
University of Virginia

The studies described in Chapters 3 to 7 represent research that examines relationships between what teachers do in classrooms (processes) and student learning (products). These studies expand typical process-product research by examining teachers' thoughts about their own teaching and about student learning. However, these early chapters do little to establish the students' perspectives. As a result, the chapters do not explore the discrepancy that frequently exists between teachers' and students' perceptions of teaching behavior, or discrepancy that is likely to disrupt communication in the classroom. This chapter reports what one mainstreamed and one typical student in the same classroom thought about the teaching practices to which they were exposed and includes, for purposes of comparison, the teacher's own account. We also discuss how these students responded to the teacher's questions, both to those which demanded factual answers and to those which required inference.

Although it seems reasonable to assume that learning-disabled students will have difficulty communicating with their teachers, there is limited documentation that records their particular difficulties. Morine-Dershimer (1982) has found that teacher praise was interpreted differently by high and low achievers, and Lepper (1983) has suggested that for some students, teacher praise could even produce results opposed to the teacher's intention. Do students with learning disabilities, we wondered, have particular difficulty with respect to interpreting teachers' intentions? Can we help teachers recognize these difficulties and prepare to anticipate them in the classroom?

A few comments about our methods of soliciting students' thoughts are in order. Because we could not observe thoughts directly, we had to rely instead on indirect measures of what was going on in students' minds as they sat in class. We rejected some of the more common approaches of obtaining information from students such as self-reports made at the end of class and paper-and-pencil survey techniques (Ahlgren, 1983). While each has its place, we found these approaches too far removed in time from students' thoughts during class. We chose instead to tap student thinking by using a slight variation of the stimulated recall procedure used with the teachers in the case studies (explained in Chapter 1). By using stimulated recall, we were able first to record students' perceptions of the same instructional events and next to compare their thoughts to the teacher's expressed intent.

PROCEDURES

Four investigators, each assigned to four different teachers, collected data on teachers' and students' interpretations of a number of behavioral events occurring during lessons. The stimulated recall procedure was essentially the same for all individuals. Each investigator showed portions of the videotaped lesson first to the teacher of the class and then to each of two students, one a mainstreamed learning-disabled student and the other a typical student. During these sessions, investigators played videotapes and audio recorders simultaneously, stopping videotapes at points of interest to ask teachers and students specific questions about the videotaped events (see Morine-Dershimer, 1983; Peterson & Swing, 1982). Teachers and students were also encouraged to stop the videotape whenever they wished to make spontaneous comments about activities of interest. All comments recorded on audiotapes were then transcribed.

To analyze teachers' and students' comments, we compared audiotaped reactions of respondents to behavioral events previously categorized in accord with behaviors in the list of effective teaching actions (see the Appendix). We calculated percentages of students' responses as either congruent or incongruent with the teachers' stated reasons for behaving as they did.

As we analyzed results from investigators' stimulated recall with teachers and students, we began to wonder whether certain kinds of questions posed special problems for the students. We explored this possibility by examining the types of questions investigators asked and the response patterns of students.

To do so, we performed a content analysis of investigators' questions to determine whether students were asked to respond to factual questions about teachers' actions or to questions that required inference about the teachers' intent. We defined inferential questions (in our minds the more difficult questions) as those that required students to draw conclusions using available evidence. Factual questions called for students to recognize or recall events.

Several assumptions affected our work. First, we believed that investigators, by videotaping on three occasions before taping for the stimulated recall sessions, could desensitize classes to their presence and prevent the undue influence of their presence upon the normal course of events in the classrooms. Second, we thought that, when viewing videotapes of lessons, teachers and students were able to remember accurately their thoughts and feelings at the time tapes were made. Third, we assumed that viewing videotapes did not distract from thinking about one's own thinking and behavior. Finally, we assumed that students could recognize and verbalize their thoughts and feelings and that both teachers and students were willing to be candid with investigators.

In this chapter, we present results from the study of one fourth-grade teacher and two of her students. Although portions from some of these sessions have been discussed briefly in Chapter 3, here we concentrate on the differences in perceptions between the mainstreamed student, Fred, and his typical peer, Tyrone. We chose these particular episodes—audiotaped reactions of the teacher and her two students to videotaped events—because they represent data collected from this classroom and also illustrate the process used to analyze data. Episodes were taken from stimulated recall sessions on a 50-minute reading lesson devoted to identifying the main idea of selected paragraphs. (Herbert and Keller discuss the context of this classroom in Chapter 3.)

Although the current presentation of episodes permits the comparison of perceptions, it is, of course, important to remember that the reflections were collected in separate viewing sessions, each involving only two people at a time—the investigator and the teacher, or the investigator and one student. The following mode of presentation juxtaposes different views of the same event so that the reader can easily compare any discrepancy.

Episode 1

The teacher asked the students to define "topic." The teacher's intent was to enhance student involvement and to check for understanding. Both Fred, the student with learning disabilities, and Tyrone were able to recognize the teacher's intent to check for understanding, but neither student perceived their teacher's attempt to gain class involvement in the lesson.

Fred	Tyrone
Investigator: What was your teacher doing here?	Investigator: What is your teacher doing now?
Fred: She was asking a question, "What is the topic?"	Tyrone: Talking about topics.
Investigator: And why was she doing that?	Investigator: Why is she asking kids to raise their hands?
Fred: To, um, whoever memorized it. Who memorized it.	Tyrone: Because she wants to find out if we know anything about topics.
Investigator: To see who had memorized it?	
Fred: Uh-huh.	

Both Tyrone's and Fred's responses convey a sense that the teacher's intent was evaluative in nature. Fred seemed to think the evaluation would determine whether students had "memorized" information. Tyrone, on the other hand, seemed to think less narrowly about his teacher's purpose when he said, "She wants to find out if we know anything about topics." To Tyrone, information about topics seemed a concept to be developed rather than facts to be memorized.

Episode 2

In this episode, after asking who could find the main idea in a paragraph written on the board, the teacher praised those with their hands raised. Immediately more hands went up. The teacher's stated intent was to "keep the kids with me, get more students involved . . . [and] encourage them to try to answer questions."

Fred	Tyrone
Investigator: Why does she say, "Good hands" ?	Investigator: Why is she saying, "Good hands" ?
Fred: Because the people know what it is.	Tyrone: Because usually people don't raise . . . all the people in the classroom don't raise their hands.

Fred's response to the investigator's question about teacher intent was limited to his perception that people who raised their hands knew the answer. Tyrone, however, seemed to understand that the teacher was trying to use praise as a stimulus to change group behavior. His perspective of teacher behavior appeared to include more information about classroom interaction, both in the present and the past.

Episode 3

After asking for a volunteer to find a main idea from a selected paragraph, the teacher, seeing Fred's willingness to answer, called on him. When Fred responded incorrectly, the teacher said, "You are almost right." As Herbert and Keller noted in Chapter 3, the teacher expressed some hesitancy to tell Fred that he was wrong. While she knew the importance of rejecting incorrect information, she was afraid of appearing harsh. How did Fred and Tyrone interpret her response to Fred?

Fred	Tyrone
Investigator: What do you think she was telling you when she said something about that was almost right? [Silence, no response] Was she trying to help you? Fred: Uh-huh. Investigator: What was she trying to help you do? Fred: Get the, um, the other answer.	Tyrone: She is telling him . . . telling him the, um, the paragraph . . . the sentence he picked out of the paragraph was good, but it didn't tell the topic out of the paragraph.

Initially, Fred appeared confused by the teacher's response. With prompting from the investigator, he was able to explain that the teacher was trying to help him get the "other" answer. Tyrone seemed to distinguish the teacher's desire to encourage Fred from her evaluation of his answer. Tyrone appeared to understand, without any prompting, that the teacher's response conveyed two different messages.

Episode 4

Confident he knew the correct answer and eager to supply it, Tyrone waved his raised hand conspicuously. The teacher thought Tyrone needed a boost in confidence and hoped to supply this boost by allowing him to answer her question.

Fred	Tyrone
Investigator: Why did your teacher call on Tyrone? Fred: He had his hand up.	Investigator: Why do you think she called on you? Tyrone: Because of my reaction . . . I guess she thought I knew it. Investigator: And what happened? Tyrone: I got it wrong, of course.

This episode, like others, illustrates Fred's tendency to interpret teacher behavior in a simplistic fashion and Tyrone's efforts to extend beyond the obvious. The episode also raises questions about whether it is helpful for students to infer the teacher's intent. In this case, Tyrone's assumption about teacher behavior was incongruent with the teacher's intent. What might happen if students were to recognize teachers' attempts to bolster self-esteem? Might students feel that they were perceived as less than able? If so, the teacher's good intentions might backfire.

Episode 5

During this episode, the teacher, who wanted to make the lesson "real," referred to a movie in an attempt to determine whether all the students could visualize a crocodile. In this way, she hoped to relate the students' experiences to her instructional objectives.

Fred	Tyrone
Investigator: Why was she talking about that movie?	Investigator: Why do you think your teacher mentioned that movie?
Fred: Because it was the main idea.	Tyrone: She wanted to . . . um . . . ask us . . . and see . . . ask us do we see a real crocodile.

Tyrone seemed to discern the relationship between the teacher's reference to a "real" crocodile and the lesson. Fred did not appear to see this connection. Instead, for Fred, the movie seemed to become the "main idea." Either he did not express himself clearly to the investigator, or he did not comprehend the reference to the film.

Episode 6

The teacher conducted a review during the lesson on the main idea. She wanted to summarize the lesson so that it would "stay with them."

Fred	Tyrone
Investigator: What is your teacher doing?	Investigator: Why is your teacher doing all this reviewing?
Fred: She wants to review.	Tyrone: Because . . . see like when she does one thing and we go on to another, she want to know do we still remember the first thing we done . . . since she done something else.
Investigator: Why is she doing that?	
Fred: So to see whoever remembers it.	

Tyrone seemed to understand that his teacher was trying to help students remember the material. Fred seemed to perceive the review as a means of evaluation.

Episode 7

While lecturing, the teacher casually walked to Fred's desk, picked up his pencil (he had just broken the lead), sharpened it, then returned it to him. In this instance, the teacher chose to sharpen the pencil rather than prompt Fred to do so. Students' sharpening pencils during the lesson "bothered" her, so the teacher did not permit such housekeeping tasks during a lesson.

Fred	Tyrone
Investigator: What is your teacher doing?	Investigator: What is your teacher doing?
Fred: Taking my pencil.	Tyrone: Took Fred's pencil I think. Oh yeah, she sharpened it.
Investigator: Why did she do that?	
Fred: I don't know. Oh, she's sharpening it.	Investigator: Why didn't she have him sharpen it?
Investigator: How come she didn't have you sharpen it?	Tyrone: She didn't want him to get up while she was reading the lesson.
Fred: I don't know.	

Tyrone seemed to understand why the teacher sharpened Fred's pencil. Fred, however, seemed somewhat confused. He merely noted the obvious ("She's sharpening it") and did not venture beyond observable facts.

Episode 8

After assigning students a workbook activity, the teacher circulated among the students. According to the teacher, she was "checking to see if [students] were doing their work . . . getting them started."

Fred	Tyrone
Investigator: What is your teacher doing?	Investigator: What is your teacher doing now?
Fred: She's, um, telling people, "Is that right?" and "That's wrong."	Tyrone: Going around. Showing people where the . . . right answer. She walking around telling where to write the sentence down on the booklet.

In this episode, both Fred and Tyrone misread the teacher's intention. From their perspective, the teacher appeared to be checking for "right" answers rather than helping students get down to business.

Episode 9

After calling on a student, Barbara, to select the main idea in a paragraph written on the chalkboard, the teacher listened to Barbara's choice but offered no response. Instead she asked, "How many of you agree with Barbara's answer?" By remaining "neutral," the teacher intended to prompt students to "think on their own" while checking to see how many students were "with her."

Fred	Tyrone
Investigator: What is your teacher doing now when she asks how many agree with Barbara?	Investigator: Why did your teacher ask if you agreed with Barbara?
Fred: Um . . . I don't know.	Tyrone: Because she wanted to . . . find out that we knew the answer. And she . . . that why she said do we agree with Barbara.
	Investigator: Did you agree with Barbara?
	Tyrone: Uh-huh.
	Investigator: Was your hand up?
	Tyrone: Yeah.

> Investigator: Your teacher said
>   something like, "I tricked you."
> Tyrone: Yeah.
> Investigator: What was your teacher
>   trying to do?
> Tyrone: Trick us.
> Investigator: Was she?
> Tyrone: And to seeing like showing
>   expressions on her face to trick us
>   to see was we really ready for
>   topics or not.

In this episode, Fred seemed to have no inkling of the teacher's intent. Tyrone recognized that the teacher was checking for understanding. Because the investigator asked Tyrone questions about the teacher's statement "I tricked you," we could also surmise that Tyrone understood the teacher's ploy of keeping her face expressionless while asking for students' reactions to Barbara's answer. We are not sure why the investigator did not ask Fred the same questions, but we assume that because Fred's response to her initial question was not fruitful, she discontinued this line of questioning. Curtailed interactions between the investigator and Fred effectively hindered further understanding of Fred's insight.

At this point it is worth noting that during our analyses of episodes, we observed that the more insightful the students' responses, the more students were questioned, challenged, and probed by the investigator. Had the investigator in Episode 9 above persisted in questioning Fred, she might have elicited insights similar to Tyrone's. Instead, Fred's lack of responsiveness seemed to put a damper on the investigator's efforts to probe for information. Other investigators, we noted, infrequently probed students, particularly learning-disabled students. It is interesting to speculate whether this restraint might be an accurate indicator of how teachers in regular classrooms are likely to respond to students like Fred.

Episode 10

At lesson's close, the teacher encouraged students to raise their hands and identify the topic of the paragraph. Few responded to this attempt to promote their involvement. In fact, several members of the class showed signs of boredom and fatigue, including Tyrone, who had his head on his desk.

Fred	Tyrone
Investigator: What do you think your teacher is thinking now?	Investigator: What do you suppose your teacher is thinking now?
Fred: I don't know.	Tyrone: Thinking everybody getting tired.
	Investigator: Why do you say that?
	Tyrone: Wasn't . . . they don't want to raise their hand.

Tyrone expressed his own feelings and seemed to embody the general fatigue. He perceived connections among the unraised hands, the teacher's failure to get the response she desired, and the teacher's attempt to alter the situation by prompting. Fred was either unable or unwilling to speculate.

RESULTS

In general, Fred's answers differed qualitatively from Tyrone's. His responses to the investigator's questions revealed his simplistic and unidimensional assessment of classroom interactions. At times, we sensed that his view of teacher behavior was limited to assessment of presently occurring events. It also appeared that Fred did not understand multiple meanings in the teacher's messages. Because Fred was mainstreamed into the regular classroom for only one hour daily, his opportunity to know the culture of this classroom was more limited than Tyrone's.

Tyrone's perceptions of the teacher's intent more closely paralleled her stated intent. His perspectives were multidimensional, encompassing more information and including past and present classroom interactions. Tyrone also appeared able to perceive dual messages and to construct inferences about the teacher's intent.

In some cases Fred's and Tyrone's perceptions differed very little. Neither student appeared to understand the teacher's attempts to enhance students' self-concepts or to attend to the special needs of a particular learner. It is unclear whether the students were unable to perceive or merely reluctant to acknowledge publicly the teacher's attempts to help students, perhaps through fear of exposing their own or classmates' academic deficiencies.

Overall, students with learning disabilities were less able than were their typical peers either to infer or to articulate teacher intent during stimulated recall sessions. Interpretations made by students with learning disabilities matched the teacher's stated intent 64 percent of the time. Typical students' interpretations matched their teachers' stated intent 72 percent of the time.[1] The content analysis also revealed that, during stimulated recall interviews, investigators reduced the frequency of inferential questions posed to learning-disabled students after receiving several incorrect responses or consecutive nonresponses ("I don't know" or silence). Students with learning disabilities were asked an average of 10 inferential questions each, whereas nondisabled students were asked an average of 26 questions each.

Predictably, both groups were better able to respond correctly to questions demanding factual answers; that is, they could accurately report what teachers did and said. Learning-disabled students and their typical peers both responded correctly to factual questions 94 percent of the time.

Inference: An Acute Problem

As Salomon (1981) observed, communications are interactive or mutually influential: poor transmission and/or poor reception on one person's part can influence the other party, contributing to a downward spiral in communications. Teachers in mainstreamed classrooms want to help their learning-disabled students. They expect communication problems, particularly when students have specific language deficits. However, they seldom know how to focus assistance. Many are unaware, for example, that inference poses acute problems for certain students. Only informed teachers can monitor their demands upon the inferential capacity of students and attempt to adjust those demands to accommodate limited interpretive ability.

Teachers also need to consider that many inferences require general knowledge of classroom culture. Mainstreamed students who are pulled out of self-contained special education classes have less access to the culture of the regular classroom than do the other students. For instance, in some recorded data, Tyrone stated that the teacher "always does that," indicating that he had a well-developed sense of the continuity of classroom events. In contrast, Fred demonstrated no such understanding.

Time spent in special education classrooms undeniably predisposes students to certain behaviors that are ill-suited to the culture of the regular classroom. The contained environment does not prepare them to compete for the teacher's attention as regular students habitually do, nor does it train them to be attentive during group instruction. In a special education classroom, the pupil-teacher ratio is considerably lower than in the regular classroom, and the individualized instructional format minimizes occasion for the teacher to address the group as a whole. As a consequence, students may be taught to tune out classroom events that do not pertain directly to them. In the self-contained setting, competing for teacher attention is seldom necessary, and attending to every teaching behavior may even be discouraged. The culture of the special education classroom is not that of the regular classroom, a fact that teachers of the mainstreamed need to recognize.

Mainstreamed students are seldom well socialized into the culture of the regular classroom; frequently they attempt to operate in ignorance of the unstated rules affecting classroom communication. Even when special education teachers try to help students acquire the mores of the regular classroom, the attempt is unlikely to succeed without complementary and collaborative effort from the regular teachers as well. Unfortunately, regular teachers are seldom prepared to deal specifically with the communication problems of the mainstreamed. Unaware of strategies for focusing assistance, teachers routinely resort to lowered expectations in a misguided attempt to alleviate communication problems.

More beneficial strategies are available to both teachers and students. John Baird and his colleagues (Baird, Fensham, Gunstone, Penna, & White, 1991) in Australia use monitoring to identify and solve classroom communication problems. Serving as mediators, they help teachers learn to state their intentions explicitly and to verify the students' understanding through joint discussion. Even students who are unable to infer meaning can then know what the teacher wants them to do. Students, for their part, learn to monitor their own attention and understanding. They are trained to ask themselves questions such as, "What is the teacher trying to do now?" or "What does the teacher want me to understand?" This self-monitoring behavior can also be tracked fairly easily so that students can learn about their own learning (Hallahan, Lloyd, & Stoller, 1982; Lloyd & Landrum, 1990).

Whatever strategies people employ to understand or improve classroom communication, those most likely to succeed will acknowledge the reciprocity of classroom life. Teachers who want to assist students with learning disabilities in their adjustment to the mainstreamed classroom will need to examine their own practices as speakers and their own demands upon the listening student. Those teachers who habitually demand inferences from students will do well to consider the limited interpretive capacity of certain students and make special provision to ensure that these students understand intended meanings.

NOTE

1. Children without disabilities answered more inferential questions correctly than did children with disabilities, $X^2=7.05$, df=1, p<.05. There were no differences between the two groups of children's correct answers to factual questions.

CHAPTER 10

Helping Teachers Reflect on Their Actions

Joanne M. Herbert
University of Virginia

In this chapter I discuss results of efforts by supervisors to intervene with teachers of mainstreamed students with learning disabilities. Interventions, structured similarly to procedures used in the case studies, required teachers to investigate their own practices through viewing and discussing videotapes of their interactions with students. During clinical episodes, supervisors were to collect teachers' thoughts about teaching and permit teachers to reconcile these thoughts with observable teaching behaviors. Supervisors were also to encourage teachers to compare their thinking and their behavior with the list of effective actions emanating from the first three case studies.

To assess the effectiveness of such assistance, four research questions were addressed

1. What are the thoughts and behaviors of teachers as they interact with students during the course of a lesson?

2. Does intervention seem to change teachers' thoughts and behaviors?

3. How do typical and mainstreamed students behave before and after their teachers receive supervisory assistance?

4. What are teachers' perceptions of the value of supervisory assistance?

One might argue that teachers who understand that their behaviors can serve different purposes also exhibit complex patterns of thought.

This position assumes that "more is better," that complexity of cognitive development is a desirable goal for teachers (Howey & Zimpher, 1996; Sprinthall & Thies-Sprinthall, 1987). One difficulty with this view is the generality of language used to communicate this idea. If supervisors and teachers are to make sense of complex actions they need concrete, classroom-relevant examples with which to work.

DESIGN

Before initial supervisory interventions with teachers, two trained observers used a low-inference instrument to collect baseline data on selected interactive teaching behaviors of four teachers over a six-week period (McNergney, Medley, & Caldwell, 1988; Medley, Rosenblum, & Vance, 1989). These behaviors—monitoring, checking for understanding, making connections, praising, approving, acknowledging, and redirecting questions—were selected because they helped define more and less effective teachers as identified by cluster analyses (Hallahan, McNergney, & McKinney, 1989).

While coding teachers' behaviors, observers also recorded the on- and off-task behaviors of two students, one a general education student and the other a mainstreamed student with learning disabilities. A weighted overall estimate of agreement (Harris & Lahey, 1978) was calculated for joint observations to determine whether observers maintained the preset standard of 70 percent agreement.

Outside the classroom, using a thought-listing procedure (Brock, 1967; Greenwald, 1968; Cacioppo & Petty, 1981), four supervisors collected data on teachers' thoughts. Four other supervisors conducted clinical interventions with the classroom teachers. This design, then, was implemented with 14 individuals: 4 teachers, 2 observers, and 8 supervisors working together in pairs.

Interventions with teachers were staggered over time; that is, clinical interventions were implemented with only one teacher at a time while baseline conditions were continued for the others. A unique feature of this design was the inclusion of a self-monitoring device (journal) that supervisors introduced to teachers during the first intervention. Daily maintenance of this journal between the first and second intervention was intended to encourage teachers to think explicitly about their actions in the classroom. This retrospective analysis apart from the pressures of performance made it possible presumably to think about the effectiveness of practice (Calderhead, 1996; Yinger & Clark, 1981).

Participants

The participants in this study fall into three groups: the teachers, the supervisors, and the observers. The four teachers who participated were faculty in two public elementary schools. The eight supervisors were all graduate students enrolled in a course on evaluation of teaching. The two observers were experienced teachers who were part-time employees of the Virginia State Department of Education.

The four teachers—two at each school—were selected because (1) they were regular classroom teachers of fourth- or fifth-grade students; (2) their reading group(s) included one or more mainstreamed students with learning disabilities who had good attendance; (3) their instructional hours and groupings for reading were consistent from week to week; (4) they had been designated by their immediate supervisors to receive opportunities for professional growth; and (5) they were willing participants. The four teachers—Sara, Mary, Brenda, and Laura—received stipends for their participation in the study.

Descriptions of these teachers in the context of their classroom settings represent data gathered from the following sources: pre- and post-intervention interviews, telephone conversations, and measures of teachers' information-processing abilities; teachers' expectations for student behavior; and teachers' assistance needs in dealing with students' behaviors (see Herbert, 1990, for a full description).

Sara

At the time of this study, Sara, a teacher with 33 years' experience, was in her tenth year as a fifth-grade teacher and her last year of teaching before retirement. She had an undergraduate degree in English and Spanish and a master's degree in fine arts. Previously, in other school systems, she had accumulated 6 years' experience as a curriculum specialist in gifted education and 22 years as a teacher of kindergarten, first-, fourth-, fifth-, and sixth-grade students.

Mary

Mary, also a fifth-grade teacher, had an undergraduate degree in English and a master's degree in elementary education. A classroom teacher with 13 years' experience, she had taught mainly at the fourth- and fifth-grade levels, although she had spent 2 of those years teaching sixth graders in a junior high school.

Brenda

Brenda, a fourth-grade teacher, had worked for 3 years as a home economist for an electric company before deciding to teach. During her 17 years as a classroom teacher, she earned a master's degree in elementary education and taught in 3 different school systems, doing both regular and resource teaching in grades kindergarten through 8.

Laura

The fourth teacher, Laura, was working in a fifth-grade classroom and had a total of 18 years' experience—8 years as a Title I teacher, 1 year as a first-grade teacher, 3 years as a fourth-grade teacher, and 6 years as a fifth-grade teacher. Enrolled at the time of the study in a master's degree program in reading, Laura had previously earned an undergraduate degree in Spanish.

Supervisors

Seven of the eight supervisors were pursuing doctorates—five in administration and supervision, one in instructional technology, and one in educational psychology. The eighth supervisor was working on a master's degree in curriculum and instruction.

All eight supervisors, four of them female and four of them male, had experience as full-time teachers, five with 10 to 13 years' experience, and three with 20 to 22 years' experience. Of the six supervisors who had taught in elementary classrooms, two had been special education teachers, one had taught both gifted and special education students, one had been a dance instructor, and two had been regular classroom teachers. Four of those with elementary experience had also taught at other levels, three at the high school level and one at the college level. Of the six with high school experience, one had taught nursing courses, two had taught English and/or developmental reading, one had taught music and English, one had taught computer classes, and another had taught students with emotional disturbances and learning disabilities.

Each pair of supervisors, comprised of a male and a female, accepted the random assignment to one of the four teachers. Assignment of their respective roles—conducting the thought listings or intervening with the teacher—was determined either by the flip of a coin or by considerations of flexibility in each supervisor's class and/or work schedules.

Observers

The two observers who collected data on teachers' interactive behaviors and the on-task involvement of students were chosen because they: (1) were blind to the experimental conditions of the study, (2) had received training from Virginia State Department of Education contractors in the use of the CPR (Classroom Performance Record) and had met or exceeded the criterion for accuracy, (3) had been trained in the method for collecting data on students' task orientation, and (4) had experience using this system in conjunction with the teacher observation form. Observers were remunerated for their work.

Instrumentation and Data Collection

To answer the four research questions, several procedures were used. For the collection of data on teachers' interactive behaviors during the instruction of reading, the trained observers used the Classroom Performance Record (CPR). Content validity for this instrument has been estimated through use of a national panel of experts asked to judge the degree to which items on the CPR reflected knowledge of effective teaching research. Evidence of construct validity has been established in several studies by correlating scores from the instrument with measures of general ability and teaching performance (Dewalt, 1986; Doss, 1987).

Using the CPR, the trained observers collected data at least three times before the first intervention and again two to three times after each of the two interventions. To do so, they recorded teacher behaviors occurring during several 3-minute segments of lessons, the number of segments being determined by the length of the lesson. (Lessons ranged from 25 to 45 minutes in length.) During collection of data on teachers' interactive behaviors, auditory cues from tape recorders also enabled observers to note the task orientation of a mainstreamed and typical student in each teacher's classroom. Under each student's name, observers marked a plus (on task) or a minus (off task) every 30 seconds, for a total of 42 or more observations per child per reading lesson.

The eight supervisors in this study either conducted interventions or gathered information on teachers' interactive thoughts. The four individuals gathering information on teachers' thoughts did so by using a thought-listing procedure. This involved showing the teacher videotapes of her own classroom teaching and asking her to write down thoughts going through her mind as she was teaching. One viewing-recording session preceded the first intervention; the other followed the second intervention. To increase the likelihood of collecting, and thus measuring, only thoughts occurring at the time of instruction, thought-listing sessions were conducted on the day when teachers were videotaped or, in the case of one supervisor hampered by weather conditions, no more than two days after the videotaping.

To collect data on teachers' perceptions of the value of clinical episodes, teachers were asked to respond in writing to several questions: (1) Were clinical episodes helpful? Why/Why not? (2) Were there any particular aspects of the interactions that you especially liked or disliked? (3) If you were to tell this supervisor how to improve his work with teachers, what would you say? and (4) How does this type of interaction compare with methods to improve teaching that are currently used in your school system? Open-ended interviews were then held with each teacher to clarify responses and to seek additional feedback about interventions.

Clinical Interventions

The four supervisors who intervened with teachers used a four-step process of clinical teacher development: (1) preplanning, (2) a preobservation conference, (3) observation and analysis of classroom behavior, and (4) a postobservation conference (McNergney & Carrier, 1981; Herbert & Tankersley, 1993). See Figure 10.1.

During the fourth step of the process, or postobservation conference, supervisors were to encourage teachers to make explicit their thoughts and behaviors occurring during lessons. To stimulate recall, teachers and supervisors viewed videotapes of lessons, sharing control of when to stop the tapes to make comments or ask questions about various interactions. Teachers were then asked to compare their actions to the effective teaching strategies listed in the Appendix.

The goal of clinical interventions was not to impose rules for teaching, but to stimulate teachers to reflect on their own actions. As Brophy and Good (1986) have argued, presenting pedagogical knowledge to teachers that is grounded in practice, and doing so in a

Figure 10.1 Clinical process for teacher education

Adapted with permission from McNergney, R. F., & Carrier, C. A. (1981), *Teacher development.* NY: Macmillan Publishing Company.

1.0	Preplanning
	—Consider teacher
	—Plan intervention strategy

2.0	Preobservation conference
	—Re-establish communication
	—Check planning (student needs and abilities, expected outcomes, and teaching strategy)
	—Describe observation process

3.0	Observation-Analysis
	—Videotape lesson
	—Examine videotape for types of interactions with students

4.0	Postobservation conference
	—View videotape
	—Question teacher about thoughts and behaviors
	—Offer instruction on teaching model
	—Discuss journal

decision-making format, allows teachers to "examine concepts critically and adapt them to the particular contexts within which they teach" (p. 370).

To encourage further introspection about their own classroom practice, teachers were also taught to keep journals with daily descriptions of factors that contributed to the success of lessons. During preobservation conferences in the second round of interventions, supervisors gave teachers opportunities to discuss their entries and their reflections on those entries.

Before conducting interventions with teachers, supervisors participated in several training sessions where they saw the four steps of the clinical process modeled and where, by role-playing with fellow supervisors, they practiced the skills needed to implement each step. Once in the field, supervisors conducting interventions audiotaped their interactions with teachers and then met with their partners, who were responsible for thought listings, to critique the audiotapes. Thus, the supervisors worked as a team, offering support and guidance to one another.

DATA ANALYSIS

1. What are the thoughts and behaviors of teachers as they interact with students during the course of a lesson?

To answer the first part of question 1 about teachers' thoughts, data recorded by teachers during thought-listing sessions were subjected to content analysis. In each case, emergent themes were verified by another independent observer (Lincoln & Guba, 1985; Erlandson, Harris, Skipper, & Allen, 1993). As will be evident in the following discussion, teachers' thoughts are described in terms of how many times thoughts were expressed during thought-listing procedures, one very simple measure of their salience. It is important to bear in mind that these totals communicate little about the complexity or origins of teachers' thoughts.

Sara

Sara, the first teacher with whom supervisors worked, recorded a total of 33 thoughts during thought-listing procedures which covered two 25- to 30-minute lessons. Content analyses revealed no thoughts focused on the mainstreamed student, 15 thoughts related to handling the content of lessons, 10 disconcerted or anxious feelings about classroom events, 5 concerns about the momentum of lessons, and 3 feelings of satisfaction about students' understanding of concepts. Examples from each of the defined categories are listed below.

A. Handling content

- "Interpreting; processing information. They [the students] need to take the various definitions of words and put them in their own words so they can handle them in an understandable context."

- "I tried to make relevant the position of the main character. I was worried they might not come up with relevant questions [so I] interjected the 5 W's."

B. Disconcerted or anxious feelings

- "I was afraid they would get me into a question I couldn't answer. But we got through it okay. I never mind saying, 'I don't know,' but I hated to do it on tape."

- "[I] fell apart here . . . [when] Paul commented . . . that he was 'happy' when he read that the Challenger blew up—typical show-off remark."

- "Understanding use of vocabulary. I make up sentences and they place the proper word in the 'blank.' I panicked when they goofed on the first one."

- "Zorro—I wasn't sure what [the students] were referring to and decided to let it pass to be on the safe side."

C. Concern for momentum

- "The reading seemed slow, but I was probably just having 'mother hen' worries."

- "[I] moved faster. I knew once they got past a certain point they would catch on and move quicker in placing coordinates."

- "Map-folding skills. I was worried they were tiring. Decided to end lesson. It *is* a two-day lesson."

D. Feelings of satisfaction

- "I was pleased how quickly they caught on. I was afraid Danielle and Ann couldn't follow, but they did quite well."

- "Coordinates: longitude and latitude. I was really surprised—pleasantly—that they got marking (tracking) the coordinates as quickly as they did."

- "Cooperative learning—make an interview with partner. Some are clowns. I was pleased some did as well as they did."

Many of Sara's thoughts, as evidenced by her choice of words, reflected fairly strong emotions. In eight thoughts, for instance, Sara described herself as "anxious," "worried," "afraid," or "nervous"; in two others she mentioned that she was "upset"; in two Sara indicated that she was "surprised" or "pleased"; and in two she said she "fell apart" or "panicked." These findings are not surprising, as both supervisors and I had noted similar emotions surfacing during our interactions with Sara. As Sara communicated to me during a preliminary interview, she found her situation quite frustrating:

> I'm looking at retirement now and I think it's a good thing . . . because I think nobody cares what's going on . . . I'd like it stricter, and I'd like someone to care about absenteeism. How can I teach them and get fussed at for not teaching them when they don't come to school . . . You know, that just bugs me . . . [and] thirty minutes is not long enough for a reading group . . . it's really pathetic . . . but you should see our schedule . . . it's nothing but dates [for assemblies]. It drives us crazy. We get very frantic about it. There's not enough teaching time . . . we move like clockwork, because right at twelve forty-five we are due in the cafeteria. And we get killed if we are one minute late . . . We have so much pressure here that it would be good to do this [study] when we are freer. Week after week the kids and I felt the strain [of being observed]. . . .

Even though these specific sources of frustration are not mentioned in the thought listings, one must consider the degree to which they possibly contributed to Sara's state of emotional well-being. It is conceivable that these and other frustrations, such as having "only ten minutes for lunch" (as she told me during one brief discussion after school), were so great that they were made manifest in the form of disconcerted or anxious feelings during teaching.

It is also important to note that Sara's thought listing was not complete and therefore may offer only a partial picture of her interactive thoughts. As Clark and Peterson (1986) have argued, and as Sara's behavior confirms, teachers often do not communicate their off-task thoughts even when instructed to do so. Following the first thought-listing procedure, for instance, Sara indicated to the supervisor that at one point during the lesson, while she was writing information for her reading students on the chalkboard, she was thinking about her daughter who was flying to her job in Florida. Sara said that she did not record this thought on the thought-listing form because it was unrelated to her reading lesson. In her way of thinking, to report off-task thoughts might make her appear less than professional in the eyes of others.

Brenda

Brenda, the second teacher with whom supervisors worked, reported a total of 59 thoughts during pre- and postintervention thought-listing sessions. Although Brenda reported more thoughts than Sara, it is important to note that Brenda's thought listings were based on two 45-minute reading lessons. Content analyses revealed that 20 of the reported thoughts were concerns about distracting behaviors of students within and/or outside the reading group; 17 were indicators of positive attention to needs, interests, understanding, and involvement of individual students; 9 reflected Brenda's efforts to "read" students' involvement and understanding; 8 were general thoughts about handling the content of the lesson; 2 were thoughts about encouraging students, 2 were judgments about the efficacy of certain teaching practices; and 1 was a description of a procedure (ritual) for dealing with students who failed to complete homework assignments. Examples of thoughts from each of these categories appear below.

A. Concerns about distracting behaviors of students within and/or outside the reading group

- "Hal doesn't want us to miss him. Hal also likes lots of attention. Snaps fingers to annoy Anna and follows camera to still be in camera's view."

- "Jonathan playing with paper. Off-task behavior of Jonathan. Asked him to behave like a student."

- "Allen runs his mouth all the time. Allen is in need of attention. He likes to monopolize the conversation and show off."

B. Positive attention to needs, interests, understanding, and involvement of individual students

- "Positive praise for work. Tasha a new student as of Friday. Very shy. Wanted to be encouraging."

- "Relating Brady's experience to picture. Using previous experience of student to see how it assists in drawing conclusions."

- "Allen not paying attention . . . called on him to get on task."

C. Reading students' involvement or understanding

- "Brady not engaged. Brady appears drugged."

- "Brady still not with us. Brady in another world."

- "Allen appears not to know. Pattern with Allen throughout year. Frequently asks for repeat of directions. Processing problems or attention-getting [behavior]?"

D. General thoughts about handling content of the reading lesson

- "Thinking time. Requested students to consider answer for about 10 to 15 seconds before called on anyone."

- "Purpose of lesson. Told purpose of lesson so students know what learning and why."

E. Thoughts about encouraging students

- "Clapping. We clapped after every student's story for positive reinforcement for writing effort."

- "Puppets. Didn't allow students to give up—gesture when arrive at correct answer."

F. Judgment about teaching practices

- "Bad example (Bob Hope.) Couldn't think of appropriate example quickly."

- "Decibels. Bad story to use. Most kids (and teacher) not familiar with range of decibels."

G. Ritual-procedure followed when homework assignments are not completed

- "Homework slip. At the beginning of each subject students who do not have assignments receive a homework slip on pressure-sensitive paper to have signed and to return the next day."

Although not one of Sara's reported thoughts was about her mainstreamed student, 16 of Brenda's were concerned with Brady, the mainstreamed student. As Brenda described him, Brady was a fairly demanding student—"a very hyperactive kid." Sara portrayed her mainstreamed student as "eager . . . into his intellectual pursuits . . . [so that] when you watch him you won't notice any difference in him, except that maybe he has a few better ideas than the others in the group."

It is also important to note that Brenda, like Sara, did not report all of her thoughts during thought-listing procedures. As she indicated to me during an informal conversation, reasons for this were twofold. First, the guarantee of confidentiality was not enough to make her comfortable with the idea of recording some of her innermost feelings, particularly her negative thoughts about students' off-task behaviors. Second, she found it difficult "to get things down on paper." According to Brenda, it was much easier to talk about her behaviors and thoughts than to record them in writing.

Mary

Mary, the next teacher to work with supervisors, reported a total of 36 thoughts during thought-listing sessions. As was true for Sara, Mary's reading lessons were shorter in duration than Brenda's: 20 minutes for the first thought-listing session and approximately 25 minutes for the second session. Subjected to content analysis, the pre- and postintervention listings included 12 thoughts about making content meaningful, 9 concerns about student involvement, 7 thoughts about helping students understand content, 4 thoughts about the momentum of lessons, 2 reactions to students, 1 concern for students' confidence, and 1 procedural observation. Examples of thoughts from each of the five categories appear below.

A. Thoughts about making content meaningful

- "Introducing lesson—concerned with explaining content (meaning of a prediction.) Link to science again—'hypothesis.'"

- "Linking to past learning. Thinking about bringing students up to date on what was covered two days ago."

- "Realization that these students have no awareness of newspaper editorials. Need to teach (explain) what an editorial is."

- "Building on student input, elaboration of students' ideas—drawing on student input to tie lesson together."

B. Concerns about student involvement

- "During oral reading thinking about monitoring students to see if all are focused on reading silently."

- "Student physical activity to focus attention to skill in lesson. Concerned with active participation from all in group to focus on task at hand—use of concrete objects."

- "Oral reading. Thinking about: Is everyone focused and on task?"

C. Thoughts about helping students understand content

- "Thinking of clarifying content for these poorer readers. This group is one year below grade level—comprehension is a struggle for many of them."

- "Workbook activity—individual quick assessment to check for understanding."

- "Rephrasing—wondering if students have understood concepts read by oral reader."

D. Thoughts about momentum

- "Thinking about time crunch—trying to telescope end of lesson and quickly finish before moving on to next lesson."

- "Need to give clear directions to students—skipping ahead in reading material."

- "Concerned with tying together divergent ideas of group and remaining on the topic—focusing toward lesson objective."

E. Reactions to students

- "Aware of classroom noise behind me—deciding whether or not to speak to noisy students."

- "Enjoying student humor which comes up in discussion."

F. Concern for students' confidence

- "Scoring answers in workbooks—to build self-confidence."

G. Observation of procedure

- "Extension with homework—extend to include a written assignment and making of airplanes for tomorrow's continuation."

Like Sara, Mary did not mention her mainstreamed student. That student, however, was absent on the day of the second videotaping.

Mary's reported thoughts were also similar to Sara's and Brenda's in that they were all task-related. Several thoughts resembled those on the list of effective teaching strategies. Her thoughts about student involvement and understanding and about the need to help students link the content of new lessons to previous lessons, for instance, seem much like categories 1, 9, and 7 in the list of effective teaching strategies (see the Appendix). Too, Mary's thoughts reflect awareness of special needs of students (see category 4 in the Appendix).

As Mary stated during an interview preceding my study, students like hers had always been "inundated with skills and workbooks and worksheets . . . , the usual boring things. . . ." She thought this unfair to students because "they never enjoy the written word . . . there's so much [emphasis] on working on finding the main idea, alphabetizing, teaching dictionary skills, and that kind of thing." Mary seemed determined to maintain a "balance," offering students "hands-on experiences" during reading instruction.

Laura

Laura's two thought listings included thoughts occurring during two 25-minute lessons. Of 36 thoughts subjected to content analysis, 11 reflected frustration or anger over distractions caused by students within and/or outside the reading group, 9 were readings of students' needs and abilities, 4 expressed feelings of uncertainty about students' abilities to understand the content of the lesson, 3 indicated concerns about the momentum of the lesson, 2 revealed feelings of joy about individual students' achievements, and 7 were unclassifiable. Thoughts in this last category seemed to be descriptions of procedures (rituals) or descriptions of teacher and student behaviors rather than representations of thoughts or feelings about either procedure or behavior. Examples for each of these categories are listed below.

A.   Frustration or anger caused by disruptive students

- "Irritated with the other group over noise level. Some kids were *not* on task and were getting on my nerves because they break the concentration."

- "MAD. Mad over the noise and activity—also that they keep making me take away from the group's time."

- "There he goes again—why doesn't Larry raise his hand?"

B.   Awareness of students' needs and abilities

- "Larry doesn't realize his miscues—Larry would keep going even if it doesn't make sense!"

- "Ray—hearing loss. [Ray said] Anna *and* Sara instead of 'Anna,' *said* Sara. Wonder if hearing loss has anything to do with it. Does he hear what he said there, or do they sound the same to him?"

- "Ramona constantly pushed to work-level. Ramona really doing well though she *always* has to struggle to keep up with group."

C.   Uncertainty about students' level of understanding

- "Someone please understand what I am saying. These children are all in LD or Title I and have trouble discussing a story—I often have to rephrase and rephrase."

- "Will Dawn answer the question—or will she panic? Dawn often just stares when you ask a question."

- "Why did I ask about the tonic? The question was posing more problems than I expected."

D.   Concerns about momentum of lesson

- "Ray needs to speed up answer. This is when Ray was answering a question and started to ramble a bit. I felt like the group was going to lose interest."

- "*We* have to get to a stopping point. We wouldn't have time to go all around the group with everyone reading a second time."

- "Larry is on a roll again. Larry starts blurting and just goes on and on at times. I was afraid he'd go on too long."

E. Joy over students' achievements

- "Derrick substantiates an answer! Yeah!"

- "Derrick starting to go beyond story [when he said] 'I wonder.' Really neat to see a Title I kid get into the story this much!"

F. Unclassifiable data

- "Trying to make eye contact with one of the other group. Lamont was 'dancing' in front of the room."

- "Larry and Roy having a side conversation. Noise—punches—hole puncher. Two punches in piece of paper in one day equals ticket to office. (Behavior management.)"

The degree to which Laura's thought listings represent her typical patterns of thinking remains undetermined. When I talked informally with her the week before her first videotaping session, Laura said things were going smoothly with the two observers, but then mentioned feeling "nervous" about the upcoming videotaping session. Laura was particularly concerned that students might "act out," an anxiety that may have caused a greater than usual attention to students' behaviors. Indeed, Laura's choice of words on thought listings reflects strong feelings about student behavior during videotaping sessions. Three times Laura described events as "getting on her nerves" or "really getting to her"; another time she merely wrote "irritation!"; and two other times she used much stronger words like "kill" to describe her feelings about student behavior (most often that of students outside the reading group).

In fact, Laura's frustration with off-task and distracting behaviors may have been no greater than usual; perhaps it was attributable to the behaviors typical within this particular group, though not to her teaching in general. This group of nine students, according to her description during an interview preceding my study, contained four students with learning disabilities (one of whom seemed "extremely hyper"), one student with an emotional disturbance, and four students designated low achievers who qualified for resource assistance through the federally subsidized Title I program.

To answer the second part of question 1—how teachers behaved during interactions with students—the trained observers using the CPR collected data 11 to 13 times in each teacher's classroom. These behaviors included

- Monitoring (visibly watching students as they worked on assigned tasks, helping individual learners, and giving step-by-step directions)[1]

- Checking for understanding during the lesson

- Making connections (relating lesson content to previous learning and/or students' experiences)

- Praising students

- Approving learners' answers or comments

- Acknowledging students' responses to questions

- Following up on student responses by redirecting the same or rephrased versions of questions to other students.

Observers were recording not the frequency, but the presence or absence of teacher behaviors during three-minute segments. Because teachers' opportunities to demonstrate behaviors were determined by the lengths of their lessons, scores for target behaviors were calculated by dividing the number of occurrences by the number of opportunities for occurrence (or the number of three-minute segments observed). To describe each teacher's behaviors, percentages of occurrence were averaged across baseline and postintervention phases to yield an overall percentage of occurrence for each target behavior.

All teachers demonstrated each of the seven target behaviors, though to varying degrees. In each case, teachers rated highest on checking for understanding, doing so in 77 percent or more of the observational intervals, and lowest on praising students, with praise occurring in 7 percent or fewer of the intervals. Although teachers seldom praised students' verbalizations, they often approved such verbalizations, clearly and explicitly indicating that a learner response or comment was correct or helpful.

2. *Does intervention seem to change teachers' thoughts and behaviors?*

To answer the first part of question 2 about teachers' thoughts, I examined teachers' thoughts before and after interventions. Interventions in the current study had been structured so that supervisors could provide teachers with a list of actions (thoughts and behaviors) demonstrated by other effective teachers. This list served not as a prescription for practice, but as a benchmark against which teachers could compare their own thinking and behaving during instruction.

Accordingly, after teachers had made their own thoughts and behaviors explicit during supervisory episodes, they were asked by supervisors to compare their actions with those on the list. My intent was to encourage teachers to move themselves toward greater complexity of action. To determine whether teachers were more complex after they had worked with supervisors, I examined their thoughts before and after interventions.

Sara

Sara had a total of 18 preintervention thoughts and 16 postintervention thoughts. As described earlier, there were five categories of thought: concern for momentum of lessons, efforts to monitor student involvement, thoughts about handling content, disconcerted or anxious thoughts, and feelings of success. Sara's postintervention thoughts reveal similar numbers of thoughts in each of the above named categories with two exceptions: nine disconcerted or anxious thoughts were recorded on the first thought listing, whereas only one appeared on the second thought listing, and feelings of success (of which there were three) appeared only during the second thought listing. Totals for other categories were as follows: handling content (seven on the first thought listing, nine on the second), and momentum (three on the first, two on the second).

The anxiety Sara seemed to reflect during the first thought listing was evident in the words she chose to describe her feelings. In eight thoughts, for instance, she used the terms "unsure," "nervous," "anxious," "panicked," or "worried." During her second thought listing, terms like "unsure," "worried," and "afraid" occurred in only three of her thoughts. It may be, of course, that Sara's first thought listing reflected more anxiety because she had been videotaped on only one prior occasion and because she was unfamiliar with thought-listing procedures. On three different occasions, twice before the first thought listing while observers were collecting baseline data, and once after the first intervention, she had asked me whether our data showed that she was "doing the right thing." Apparently, involvement in this project made her somewhat uneasy, and the absence of response from researchers, committed by their experimental design to withholding their responses except during interventions, may actually have contributed to her anxiety.

Differences between Sara's pre- and postintervention thoughts may also have been due to effects of interventions. For example, after the second intervention, in the category pertinent to handling content, were three thoughts qualitatively different from thoughts following the first intervention. These correspond quite closely with category 1 in the list of effective teaching strategies (see the Appendix). Also, after the second intervention Sara talked about "multidisciplining" in her teaching, a concept apparently similar to category 7 in the list.

Even though the intervention may have stimulated Sara to think about these things, I do not know whether she learned these ideas from the supervisor or whether she simply recalled them from other past experiences. Most likely, given her level of experience and education, she had encountered these ideas before working with the supervisor. In fact, Sara's past experience and knowledge of best practice was apparent, and at times she appeared eager to rely on her own judgment even when it ran contrary to others' ideas. For instance, during her postintervention thought listing she wrote, "I knew I should have closure but it felt redundant at this point . . . we will review again as we begin tomorrow."

Even if the clinical intervention only prompted Sara to recall past experience and to consider best practice, one might argue that this consequence was worth the effort on the part of the supervisor. Indeed, one purported benefit of clinical or "job-embedded" interventions is that they help teachers stretch their thinking beyond generalities to consider conditions of teaching and learning in their own classrooms.

Brenda

The number of thoughts reported by Brenda during pre- and postintervention thought-listing procedures was remarkably consistent: 29 and 30, respectively. As discussed earlier, each thought fell into one of six categories

1. Positive attention to the needs, interests, and involvement of students

2. Thoughts about handling content

3. Thoughts about encouraging students

4. Concerns about behaviors of students within and/or outside the reading group

5. Doubts about the efficacy of certain of her teaching practices

6. A description of procedures (rituals)

Comparison of Brenda's two thought listings reveals 12 thoughts indicative of positive attention to students' needs, interests, understanding, and involvement on the first listing and 5 on the second listing. Thoughts relative to distracting behaviors of students also appeared on both thought listings. The 7 reported on the first listing all pertained to behaviors of students outside the reading group. In contrast, of the 14 on the second listing, 6 pertained to students outside the group, 7 were thoughts about behaviors of students within the group, and 1 expressed concern about the influence of a student outside the group on a student within the reading group. Specific thoughts pertinent to handling content, encouraging students, and conducting procedure (ritual) appeared only on the first thought listing. Occurring only on the second listing were thoughts about assessing students' involvement and about the efficacy of teaching strategies.

There were some differences in Brenda's pre- and postintervention thoughts, particularly with regard to Brady, the mainstreamed student. On her first listing Brenda recorded 4 thoughts about Brady, with each thought reflecting positive attention to Brady's needs, ability, or understanding. Brenda's second thought listing contained 12 thoughts about Brady, 3 indicating positive attention to Brady's involvement, 7 representing attempts to judge Brady's involvement or understanding (similar to category 1 of the effective teaching strategies), and 2 thoughts about Brady's off-task behaviors.

There were more instances on the first videotape of off-task behavior from students in the reading group than on the videotape from the second session. Brenda's reaction in the first videotape as expressed in her thought listing was to ignore much of the off-task behavior of students in her reading group. In the second videotape, as in her second thought listing, Brenda was more attentive to such behavior. During instruction she was quick to respond to off-task behavior, frequently pulling students back into the lesson by asking a content-related question or reprimanding them for their inattention.

Mary

Mary had a total of 16 preintervention thoughts and 20 postintervention thoughts, categorized as follows: concerns about making content meaningful, thoughts about the involvement of students, concerns about the momentum of lessons, reactions to students, concern for students' confidence, and descriptions of procedures. With the exception of four thoughts (one on the first listing concerning students' confidence, one describing a homework assignment, and two thoughts on the second listing reflecting Mary's reactions to noise and student humor), Mary's pre- and postintervention thoughts were quite similar.

There were, for instance, two thoughts on each of the listings reflecting concern about the momentum of lessons, four thoughts on the first listing and five on the second about student involvement, four on each listing indicating concern for students' understanding, and four on the first listing and seven on the second regarding making lesson content meaningful.

Despite these similarities, thoughts on the second listing suggest that Mary was more attuned to needs of individual students than she was during the first thought listing. This interpretation is supported by her thought about involving Joe, "a quiet student," and also by her two thoughts about the involvement of another student, Brandy.

Laura

There were 15 thoughts on Laura's first thought listing and 21 on her second listing. Each thought was classified according to one of the following categories: concerns about the momentum of the lesson, frustration or anger over distractions caused by students within and/or outside the reading group, uncertainty about students' level of understanding, feelings of joy about students' achievements, readings of students' needs and abilities, and descriptions of procedures or teacher and student behaviors.

Both listings included thoughts reflecting anger or frustration about students' behavior (five on the first listing and six on the second) and thoughts descriptive of procedures or teacher/student behaviors (three on the first thought listing, four on the second). The three thoughts indicating concern about the momentum of the lesson and the four reflecting uncertainty about students' abilities to understand appeared only on the first listing, whereas the nine readings of students' needs and abilities and the two thoughts showing feelings of joy about students' achievements were all recorded on the second thought listing.

Laura's thought listings, like those of the other teachers, indicate that interventions had a positive effect on teachers' thoughts. In Laura's case, comparison suggests that she was more attuned to the needs, abilities, and progress of individual students on the second thought listing than on the first listing.

To answer the second part of question 2—whether supervisors were able to move teachers' behaviors toward a model of effective teaching—researchers plotted percentages graphically for each teacher across baseline and intervention phases (see Herbert, 1990, for a complete description of these results). Graphed data were then evaluated through "visual inspection" for systematic intervention effects.

Figure 10.2, for example, illustrates teachers' uses of monitoring behaviors. An examination of patterns of behavior in Figure 10.2 reveals that interventions had no obvious effect on the monitoring behaviors of Sara and Brenda but perhaps a slight effect on those of Mary and Laura. In Mary's case, monitoring behavior occurred in 10 to 24 percent of the observation intervals during the baseline phase, then, directly after the interventions, increased to 33 percent. After each postintervention increase, however, percentages of occurrence fluctuated greatly, with most data points either falling below or overlapping those in the baseline phase. This variability makes it difficult to determine whether changes in monitoring resulted from the supervisors' interventions.

In Laura's baseline phase, mean occurrence for monitoring was 14 percent, with percentages ranging between 0 and 28. Following the first intervention, mean occurrence increased to 41 percent, with both data points well above baseline levels. This increase in level, however, did not hold for observations following the second intervention. Here mean occurrence dropped to 10 percent, with data points (7 and 10 percent)

Figure 10.2 Percentage of intervals across baseline and postintervention phases during which teachers monitored (visibly watched students, gave step-by-step directions, helped students).

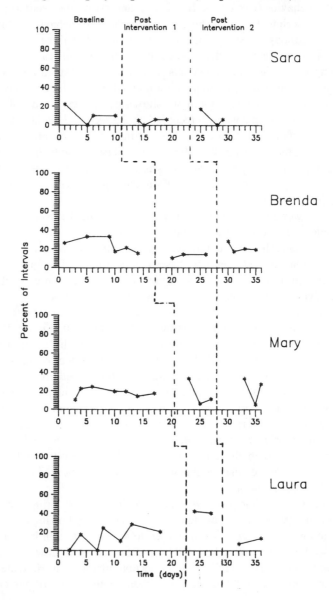

reverting to baseline levels. This inconsistency in behavior from one intervention phase to the next made it difficult to draw inferences about intervention effects, particularly since there were so few data points after interventions. Effects may have been due to history, maturation, or boredom with the project.When data on teachers' use of questioning (checking for understanding) were plotted, data points on graphs for Sara, Mary, and Laura tended to overlap from one phase to another, an overlap which indicated that interventions had little effect on the three teachers' use of questioning. Data points in Brenda's baseline phase fluctuated between 50 and 89 percent, but following the first intervention, appeared to stabilize and also increase in level with all points falling between 86 and 100 percent. Following the second intervention, however, occurrence dropped dramatically, fluctuated between 33 and 83 percent, and showed a slight downward trend. It was difficult to determine, therefore, whether the first intervention contributed to behavioral changes, because data points in the baseline phase hinted at an upward trend in occurrence.

Occurrences of behaviors during questioning—praising, approving, acknowledging, and redirecting questions—appeared unaffected by interventions. Data points for praise were consistently low; those for approving, acknowledging, and redirecting not only fluctuated greatly but overlapped across baseline and intervention phases.

Similarly, data regarding teachers' attempts to relate lesson content to previous learning and/or students' experiences indicated no upward trend after interventions. In all cases, data points were variable and overlapped across phases. For the most part, then, teachers' performances on the seven target behaviors showed no systematic changes which could be attributed to supervisors' interventions.

3. *How do typical and mainstreamed students behave before and after their teachers receive supervisory assistance?*

To answer the third question, percentages of on-task involvement for each targeted student were plotted graphically across baseline and postintervention phases. Evaluations of the data revealed no variations in student behavior clearly attributable to interventions. Percentages of on-task involvement were consistently high across all phases for both of Sara's students, and except for two data points, quite high for Mary's mainstreamed and typical students. On-task involvement of Brenda's and Laura's students was also fairly high but was more variable than that of either Sara's or Mary's students. This finding was not surprising, as both Brenda's and Laura's thought listings suggested that off-task behavior troubled them more than it did Sara and Mary.

4.   *What are teachers' perceptions of the value of supervisory assistance?*

To answer this question, I examined teachers' responses to a follow-up questionnaire about the value of working with the supervisors on this project. I also talked with teachers at the end of the study to collect additional information about their perceptions of the project. Overall, teachers were quite positive about the experience.

Sara

Sara responded to the questionnaire saying:

> Yes [this was helpful]. Anytime you are made to focus on strategies
> and responses, it is beneficial. Rhea [the supervisor] could point to
> some things I had not noticed.

Sara's responses during the follow-up interview further explicated her thoughts about the benefits of this particular method of intervention. She noted that the clinical process made her look at herself more critically, noticing her tone of voice, for example. Through videotapes of her instruction she could also observe such patterns of behavior as her tendency to slow down to get students' attention, a behavior which she had worried might make things boring but which, as the videotapes indicate, did not appear to have that effect. Interventions also helped Sara see her students in a different way, resulting in attempts to try and "draw them out." Furthermore, she felt that observations kept her "on the ball," causing her to "liven up" her instruction.

Brenda

When I talked with Brenda at the end of the project, she expressed disappointment that her supervisor had not pointed out any of her weaknesses, but she thought the interventions had been helpful. In addition to her increased awareness of students' behaviors, Brenda noted that the videotapes had enabled her to notice what two of her more difficult students (one of whom was the mainstreamed student) were doing while she was teaching. The tapes also stimulated her to think about how she might change the seating arrangement at the reading table. Brenda also said that her supervisor made the kinds of suggestions she would have expected; that is, the supervisor concentrated on effective teaching strategies like those stressed in her school system's career ladder program.

Brenda's responses to the questionnaire were equally positive:

> It was beneficial to review the lesson from the "outside." I was able to get a different perspective on the dynamics of the group . . . I prefer this approach because it allows the evaluator and the teacher to view together the videotaped episode and discuss ideas and insights on specific incidents throughout the lesson. This evaluation procedure seems to personalize the process and make it less perfunctory.

Mary

Mary, like Sara and Brenda, was positive about clinical episodes. During the informal interview Mary credited work with her supervisor for helping her see her students from another perspective. Mary's responses to the questionnaire elaborate on this idea:

> The clinical episodes were helpful in focusing on various specific aspects of each taped lesson. They were informative, for example, because of Sam's [the supervisor's] questions about certain students and particular behaviors exhibited during segments of the lesson. These questions helped me to make further inquiry into or evaluations about some students in the group . . . While teachers and observers frequently engage in discussions about a lesson which has been taught and evaluated, it is helpful to have the lesson available for replay and further scrutiny as decisions are made to improve teaching. . . . It was a rare opportunity—an interesting and enlightening one—to see oneself as others see us and to see our students from a different, more revealing, perspective. I definitely found this to be a professional growth experience.

Laura

When I talked with Laura at the end of the study, she noted that videotapes had helped her realize the importance of eye contact with her students, particularly Ramona, the target mainstreamed student. Laura also said, however, that intervening two times had not been enough—that she would have been more receptive to her supervisor's ideas if she had worked with him over a longer period of time. She described the interventions as "interesting," but somewhat disconcerting because her supervisor had not noted some of the behaviors that Laura felt she had demonstrated during lessons. Laura added that the list of effective teaching strategies shared by her supervisor was similar to recommended practices for teachers participating in the school system's career ladder program. According to Laura, she already had such practices in mind and preferred to think of them as "second nature." Had the supervisor been her principal, Laura said, she would have challenged him on some of his perceptions of her interactions with students. As Laura's response to the questionnaire indicates, she seemed most concerned with her immediate and observable behaviors:

> I liked the opportunity to see myself teach. I was amazed at how differently I came across on camera compared to how I *thought* I was coming across. I felt like I smiled more and was surprised at how little I actually did! Also, seeing what you missed during the group was a real eye-opener!

RESULTS AND DISCUSSION

This study involved the use of a rather complicated procedure for examining the effectiveness of supervisory episodes with teachers. While I studied only four teachers and my results therefore are not definitive in any sense, the findings raise a number of questions that merit further consideration in both research and practice.

For instance, when assessing the effects of experimental treatments, what kinds of data are most important? In my study, there was little or no evidence that the methods of the procedure could be validated in terms of teachers' interactive behaviors or in terms of the in-class behaviors of students. In all cases, however, there were differences in teachers' pre- and postintervention thoughts that might be attributable to interventions. Self-report data from teachers also suggest that the methods of observing and giving feedback were helpful to teachers for a variety of reasons. Which of these results are we to put most stock in when assessing the effects of clinical interventions?

Furthermore, how much of a change is enough to conclude that supervisors have affected teachers, and teachers, in turn, have influenced students? We have tests for determining the statistical significance of results, but what might we do to assess the educational significance of such changes? Teachers seemed more attuned to the needs, abilities, and progress of individual students on the second thought listing than on the first listing, but these differences in thinking are not reflected in their outward behaviors. What does this mean for practice? Must changes in thoughts precede changes in behaviors or vice versa?

It is also important to ask whether we can assume all prospective and practicing supervisors or administrators are equally adept at helping teachers think and behave to the fullest of their abilities. Are some supervisors so predisposed to tell teachers what constitutes "best practice" that they are unable to encourage teachers to examine teaching for themselves? An investigation of transcripts from clinical episodes suggests that, on the surface, supervisors were very similar in the kinds of things they discussed during postintervention conferences with teachers. There were, however, qualitative differences in their verbalizations that made some supervisors appear more effective in their efforts to encourage teachers to think about their actions per se and in relation to the list of effective teaching practices (Herbert & Tankersley, 1993).

When Mary's supervisor demonstrated active listening or encouraging/praising behaviors, for example, his comments were not ends in themselves (as they typically were for Laura's supervisor). Instead, he often used his remarks as springboards for probing Mary's thoughts about situations or events—in a sense modeling how to be reflective while communicating that he valued Mary's perspective. At the end of clinical interventions, he also asked Mary to compare her own actions to those of other teachers. In contrast, Laura's supervisor "told" her how she compared with other teachers.

Finally, can we assume that all teachers will be able to reflect on their actions even with supervisory support? Laura noted at the end of clinical sessions that she needed more practice with this particular method of self-investigation—"twice was not enough." If time is a crucial factor, is it reasonable to assume that supervisors, with the many tasks they must perform, will be able to allocate the time necessary for fostering reflection among teachers? Answers to these questions may help us maximize the benefits from the limited opportunities for supervisor-teacher interaction that now exist.

NOTE

1. This definition of monitoring evolved from factor analyses of the CPR (McKinney, 1987).

CHAPTER 11

Working Together to Help Teachers and Students

Robert F. McNergney, Daniel P. Hallahan,
Stanley C. Trent, and *Jill C. Hockenbury*
University of Virginia

This final chapter offers an opportunity to look back at what we have learned about teaching and learning in mainstreamed classrooms and to look forward toward helping teachers work with students with learning disabilities in similar situations. In doing so we undertake four tasks. First, we re-examine our assumptions about teachers and about ourselves as researchers, noting how our views have changed over the course of the project; these changes have had implications for both the conduct and interpretation of our work. Second, we review what we hoped to achieve when we began these investigations. Third, we review what we learned and discuss the value of these interrelated investigations. And fourth, we describe what needs to be done to stretch our own and others' thinking about teaching students who need special help in classrooms throughout the land.

OUR ASSUMPTIONS

We began as a group of people with concerns about teaching, learning, and teacher education. As professionals, we came to the project with primary training and interests in two areas: special education and general education. Only as time and work progressed did we approach what might reasonably be called a "team," and even then members came and went. Although at times we reflected some fairly sharp philosophical differences, we always were concerned collectively about the needs and abilities of hard-to-reach children and about the challenges these children present to their teachers.

We assumed that teachers, like students, are different from one another and that such differences have implications for how they learn. This is a familiar refrain for some of us, but one with almost limitless variations. We also believed, however, that most teachers do not learn much by being told what to do, regardless of how wise the advice might be.

People, books, and programs all advocate particular views about teaching and learning, but most teachers most of the time benefit from active intellectual involvement with their own problems. There was no question in our minds that the demands placed on teachers vary greatly. While teachers bring different abilities to classrooms, they are shaped personally and professionally by the situations in which they work.

Since the early 1970s, Joyce and Weil (1972) have helped teachers and teacher educators see these situations not only for what they are, but for what they can be. They have guided many away from "modeling the master" and toward "mastering the model" of teaching, or more precisely, the models of teaching. Because they recognize that no single way of teaching is appropriate with all students for all purposes, they taught people how to enrich teaching repertoires to include a variety of strategies that have fit different students in various situations. The wisdom of the approach is obvious; the path to success, however, is obscure.

We continue to believe that one of the primary ways teachers learn from their experiences is through imitation of others they perceive as more competent. Teachers, although they seldom benefit from being told what to do, frequently learn by observing what to do. Teachers, like other professionals and skilled craftspeople, have much to gain from watching and listening to others.

Although imitation need not place the observer-imitator in a subservient role, our egalitarian instincts and our anti-model-the-master outlook might sometimes inhibit our abilities to learn from those we observe. Polanyi (1964) put it forcefully:

> An art which has fallen into disuse for the period of a generation is altogether lost. There are hundreds of examples of this to which the process of mechanization is continuously adding new ones. These losses are usually irretrievable. It is pathetic to watch the endless efforts—equipped with microscopy and chemistry, with mathematics

and electronics—to reproduce a single violin of the kind the half-literate Stradivarius turned out as a matter of routine more than 200 years ago.

To learn by example is to submit to authority. You follow your master because you trust his manner of doing things even when you cannot analyze and account in detail for its effectiveness. By watching the master and emulating his efforts in the presence of his example, the apprentice unconsciously picks up the rules of the art, including those which are not explicitly known to the master himself. These hidden rules can be assimilated only by a person who surrenders himself to that extent uncritically to the imitation of another. A society which wants to preserve a fund of personal knowledge must submit to tradition. (p. 53)

Tradition held powerful sway over our own activities. Our shared view of research and of ourselves as researchers early in the life of the project would identify us as logical positivists. All of us were fairly well steeped in this tradition of research, and the canon served our purposes, or so we believed. To be sure, some of us were more logical and some more positivist than others, but we all seemed to ascribe our methods and procedures to notions of cause and effect and to our belief in the power of empirically derived interventions to solve educational problems. Like other educational researchers, even those who publicly eschew "scientific," "objective," inquiry, most of the members of our team were social reconstructionists: we have been and remain intent on making schools better places to be.

We suspect we grew more pragmatic during the course of the project. Certainly our research design pushed us in that direction—from behavioral observation of a group, through a series of case studies, to democratically organized and delivered interventions with teachers. We moved rather quickly away from concepts of "variable," "control," "error," and the like, to concerns about full and fair representation of behaviors and thoughts. We did not want to sacrifice asking what we thought were the most important questions because of an inability to place them in a tightly controlled research design. As time passed, we put more effort into trying to make sense out of connections between what people said, did, and thought. And we tried to interpret people's actions in relation to one another.

To describe these changes in our view and approach as a metamorphosis or as a full-fledged Kuhnian paradigm shift would be stretching a point and certainly would make the evolution sound more elegant than it was. We know ourselves well enough to be skeptical of our own abilities to cast off old ideas and to integrate new ones. Maybe, as Lippman (1913) observed many years ago, what really happened during the course of the project was that our own autobiographies crept into our work: we thought more about what teaching and learning meant to us personally.

WHAT WE HOPED TO LEARN

Approaching the research project as rationalists led us to want to find out certain facts. Our goal was to come up with an orderly set of findings that would reveal at least a piece of the *truth* about what makes teachers effective in working with mainstreamed students with mild learning disabilities. We were searching for identifiable clusters of teachers, and we wanted these clusters to be related to the on-task behavior of the mainstreamed students. We hoped our results would allow us to predict which teachers would be the best candidates for teaching students with mild disabilities. We sought to change the actions of teachers in the ineffective clusters to fit more closely the actions of effective teachers, thereby increasing their effectiveness with students possessing mild disabilities. We would also have been pleased to demonstrate some change in students' behaviors.

Having conducted field-based research in the past, we were aware that numerous pitfalls along the way would threaten validity of our data and would plague our rational efforts. We were not expecting to find clusters that were mirror images of each other, to achieve significance levels of .0001 in all our MANOVAS, or to turn every miserable teacher into a Socrates. None of us, however, expected we would find as many impediments to our efforts as we did.

Our own choice on instrumentation contributed an unremitting source of irritation. Before the project, we viewed the Continuous Performance Record (CPR) of the Beginning Teachers' Assistance Program, the main instrument we used for the quantitative portion of the project, as a particular strength, because it would allow us to relate our data to those collected on several hundred beginning teachers throughout the state of Virginia. Factors intrinsic to the instrument, as well as the cultural context in which we operated, however, created several critical problems for us. The CPR was constructed for the purpose of evaluation rather than research. The method of scoring the on-task behavior of students of the teachers in the beginning teacher sample was not so precise as we would have liked. On the original CPR, observers provided a retrospective estimate of the percentage of time when the entire class was on task for the previous three-minute time period. We added our own assessment of on-task behavior which required observers to note every 10 seconds whether an individual student was on or off task. This modification of the CPR allowed us to collect more useful data on our sample, but it did not solve the measurement problems pertaining to the beginning teacher sample.

The evaluative nature of the instrument also made teachers, who viewed it with distrust and suspicion, reluctant to be observed. Although we tried to assure them we would not disclose individual results to anyone, many of them, we believe, refused to participate for fear of disclosure. In fact, some teachers may have declined because there was such widespread antagonism toward the Beginning Teachers Assistance Program and thus toward the CPR.

WHAT WE LEARNED

We learned that good teachers in classrooms with mainstreamed learning-disabled students behave interactively with students in some clearly identifiable ways. They watch students as they work; give step-by-step directions; give hints and clarify misunderstandings; take into account learners' special needs; summarize and review throughout a lesson; connect what is to be learned to students' interests, to the outside world, and to other subject matter; prod students to answer or make comments; check understanding throughout the course of a lesson; question students and respond to their answers in a variety of ways; and build students' self-concepts by encouraging their participation and success. To be sure, some of these teaching behaviors are more easily observable than others, but collectively they yield the image of the teacher as an active agent in students' learning. This image, sketched as it is from behavioral observation, is a rough outline of teaching effectiveness that may guide teachers and teacher educators in their efforts to improve instruction.

As we moved beyond direct low-inference observation of teachers in classrooms to explore teachers' thoughts about their work, we began to expand this outline. We learned that similar instructional behaviors may proceed from quite different reasoning and that such reasoning is not always apparent.

Teachers' efforts to "make connections" between subject matter and students' interests, the outside world, and other subjects is a good case in point. Teachers engaged in such activities because they wanted to enhance student attentions and to stimulate student interest in the material under consideration; when new material was tied to familiar material, teachers believed such possibilities for learning were increased. Teachers also wanted to make the content real or meaningful, almost as if they were attempting to create images in their students' minds. As they tried to link subjects with one another, teachers wanted to ease the learning of new material by helping students perceive overlap among subjects—"Don't be overwhelmed, you are familiar with these ideas." And by forging connections, teachers hoped to anchor what was new to what had already been learned.

Understanding why teachers behave as they do is at least as important if not more so than documenting how they behave. If we can discern the thinking underlying observable action, we might be better able to predict how people will behave when they are placed in the position of teacher. We might also be able to help teachers recognize how their thinking can impede or facilitate what they do, and how their students' thinking and behavior are affected as a result.

We learned that teachers conceived of their personal and professional roles in various ways. As the individual case studies and Ellwein's meta-ethnography indicate, teachers' images of themselves— teacher as author, as survivor, as manager, as leader, as supervisor, as confident struggler—did not simply reflect their classroom lives; these images shaped how teachers behaved. We can only speculate about the long-term effects of these mental images on teachers in general. But it seems highly plausible that teachers' conceptions of themselves may figure into how long they stay on the job and how effective and satisfied they are while they are there.

We learned that the students with disabilities we observed had difficulty inferring teachers' intentions and expectations. More often than typical students, they simply misunderstood teachers' stated intentions. At other times they did not or could not speculate about what teachers meant or what teachers aimed to do. These students' misunderstandings and linear responses seemed to "pull" interviewers to ask less of them. One can only wonder if teachers are affected likewise.

We learned that teachers liked working with supervisors who listened to them and asked questions about reasons underlying their classroom behaviors—supervisors who encouraged reflection. We also learned that supervisors were more and less effective at encouraging teachers to reflect on their behaviors. Some supervisors could help teachers decenter and consider their teaching in light of a model of effective practice that was not part of their normal repertoire. These supervisors asked teachers questions about teaching behaviors instead of telling teachers what they saw or what they thought teachers should do. Teachers' feelings toward these supervisors may have been no more than a reaffirmation of the Hawthorne effect—the effect of having somebody, anybody, observe—but the positive effect may also provide a clue to the importance of involving teachers intellectually in teaching and learning.

In support of this contention, we noticed on many occasions that when the evaluative aspects in all phases of our project were low, participation was high. Our own team members, teachers in the clustering studies, principals, parents, students in the series of case studies, and teachers and supervisors in the interventions study gave willingly of their time and energy when it appeared they felt involved in the work. We believe this élan, created by freedom from the heavy hand of control, may have more to do with successful educational intervention than others have previously acknowledged. There is ample evidence to suggest that children who approach intellectual matters in an involved, independent fashion are more likely to learn than those who are coerced to do so. It would be ludicrous to think teachers are different. The zeitgeist of regulation which dictates that teachers be "held accountable" at every turn may do much more to stimulate hostility than it does to advance teachers' professional participation in educational life.

We learned, almost as an aside, that the general education teachers with whom we worked had little or no contact with special education personnel who might have provided supervisory assistance. Our own supervisors in the intervention study were outsiders assigned to help teachers think about their teaching in a mainstreamed setting; they were in no position to take ownership of teachers' problems or to work in a stable collaborative relationship with the teachers to foster change. Our supervisors and other project team members noticed, however, that teachers did not mention any past contacts with special educators vis-àvis the mainstreamed students, nor did teachers even speculate about future contact.

WHAT NEEDS TO BE DONE

Mainstreaming spreads through district classrooms at different rates, from very gradually to total district conversions within a few years. The National Association of State Boards of Education (1995) describes the different ways school districts embrace mainstreaming: "Some districts report using an 'evolutionary' process—that is, as individual parents request that their child be mainstreamed into the general education class, the district accommodates the request" (p. 15). The principal advantage of this approach is that the transition is gradual and very smooth. By mainstreaming students on a case-by-case basis, teachers and building administrators are not "scared off" by the change process. Mainstreaming students in an ad hoc fashion, however, does not force a district to consider how the system must be realigned—that is, how funding mechanisms, testing and grading policies, teacher hiring and evaluation, and staff assignments must be realigned.

Districts that work on mainstreaming by initiating special pilot programs, usually funded through special project grants, are next on the continuum. The pilot program usually provides administrators with evaluation data that can be used to "sell" the program. Pilot sites can serve as prototypes for district personnel to visit as part of the education and communication stages of the planning process. Typically, administrators implement model mainstreaming programs, selecting only highly effective general or special education teachers to pilot the programs. They provide these teachers with rewards for their willingness to participate in the programs (e.g., assistance from paraprofessionals, additional instructional materials and supplies, and special in-service training). Often more attentive to pilot programs than to established programs, administrators are willing to make special allowances to help ensure success for the new program. Many of these special provisions are relatively subtle, but they can make all the difference between success and failure. The scheduling of classes to ensure that instruction is maximized is but one example. Many established mainstreaming programs are subverted by scheduling conflicts between general and special education classes.

Over the years, model mainstreaming programs have failed to recognize hidden factors that affect the spirits of participating teachers.

Designation as a "model teacher," constant classroom visits, and having one's classroom held up as an example of effectiveness can hardly fail to provide social reinforcement to participating teachers. Regrettably, when attempt is made to extend a pilot program to other classrooms, special rewards and provisions are removed, previously uninvolved teachers are expected automatically to engage in the new program without original support and incentives, and—not surprisingly— programs often fail.

Other districts "phase in" mainstreaming in a comprehensive but gradual manner, with the explicit understanding that within a certain period of time all students will be mainstreamed in age-appropriate classrooms in the school they would normally attend. In some districts, mainstreaming is phased in grade by grade, usually starting with prekindergarten and kindergarten and adding the next one to two grades each year. In these cases, all students begin school in classrooms of diverse learners and continue in mainstream settings as they proceed through their school careers.

Some districts have blended two of the previously mentioned methods, while others have instituted a mainstreaming policy on a districtwide basis, making the complete change in a period of one or two years. These tend to be districts that are used to operating flexibly, have a small central administration, and a very open staff and community.

Salend, Brooks, and Salend (1987) surveyed educators responsible for coordinating their school districts' mainstreaming programs to ascertain the degree to which their programs incorporated the elements that contribute to successful mainstreaming programs. While districts have acknowledged a commitment to the philosophy of mainstreaming, few districts had systematic and viable procedures to ensure its implementation. Much of the implementation of mainstreaming appears to be based on informal networks between regular and special educators within individual schools rather than on established policies.

If mainstreaming is to be as effective as we would hope, we need to understand not only how teachers' thoughts and behaviors fit together, and how teachers' actions affect students, but also how all the key education players can collaborate to promote student success. Indeed, time and money are too precious to do otherwise. Many of the same constraints that impeded the initial enforcement of the Education of the Handicapped Act in 1975 still affect the implementation of innovative mainstreaming involving collaborative action. These constraints are apparent in schools and in both preservice and in-service preparation of teachers.

Teacher education programs have promoted, and then abandoned, one service delivery option after another whenever expected outcomes were not realized. As Kauffman and Pullen (1989) argue:

> We have been too quick to imagine a remedy, too slow to recognize a nostrum, and too eager to abandon a strategy because it is not a panacea. In our inevitable disappointment with each new service delivery plan, we have invariably compounded our errors by exaggerating and overgeneralizing both its promise and limitations. Currently popular and emerging service delivery models seem destined to the same fate as their immediate predecessor, the self-contained special class, partly because of the untethered ardor of their proponents. (p. 13)

In practice, mainstreaming means different things in different educational settings and districts, and can take many forms. From studies of schools ranging from preschools to high schools, from rural to suburban to urban, and in wealthy districts as well as poor ones, mainstreamed children are served in different ways. Most educators and key personnel realize that whatever service delivery model is established (e.g., co-teaching between general and special education teachers, consultation/collaboration models), needs should be continually evaluated and adjusted. The fine-tuning of these models and the procedures for implementation must be considered with particular academic and social outcomes in mind for students with disabilities. One "right" mainstreaming model that is effective across school sites does not exist. Each site must develop unique service delivery models for its students with learning disabilities that reflect the needs of the students in that school and the expertise and beliefs of key individuals, particularly teachers.

According to Hallahan, Kauffman, and Lloyd (1996), the mainstreaming network should function as an interactive team, sometimes referred to as a collaborative team, where all members work together to achieve a common goal and share their expertise and perceptions with others. In the collaborative consultation model, for example, special educators serve as consultants to general education teachers, collaborating with them in planning and implementing instructional accommodations in as many as 10 or more general education classrooms. Typically, students with learning disabilities are dispersed throughout many classes and are not clustered in particular ones.

By rotating among classrooms, special educators help teachers assess and instruct a variety of students, those identified with disabilities and those identified as being at risk. Depending on the situation, special educators may do such things as provide special materials, assist a teacher in developing special materials, provide assistance in task analysis (leading to modified instructional ideas), or develop student contracts. Such assistance may be relatively direct or indirect (Gearheart, Weishahn, & Gearheart, 1996).

There are two major components in the collaboration and consultation model. These include consultation, where special education teachers "consult" with other school personnel, and collaboration, where all educators collaborate in providing programs to students with disabilities. While consultation is the multidisciplinary planning aspect of the model, collaboration is the multidisciplinary cooperative teaching that results from the planning. Presently, consultation and collaboration are used together to describe the way interactions occur when providing services to students with disabilities in general education classes. For this model to be successful, all parties involved in the collaborative effort must be viewed as equally capable of helping students with disabilities. Success in developing an atmosphere of parity requires all professionals to enter into the collaboration/consultation model with the mind-set that all team members share equal responsibility for students, and have important and unique contributions to make to the process (Smith, Polloway, Patton, & Dowdy, 1995).

Another flourishing service delivery plan is the co-teaching approach in which the general and special educators team to offer instruction, sharing the teaching for a single group of students, typically in a single classroom setting. Both teachers share leadership in the classroom and are engaged equally in the instructional activities. Co-teaching has become a celebrated strategy, because it combines the strengths of the general education teacher and the special education teacher in creating many options for instructional delivery. For example, two teachers may role-play how to conduct an effective writing conference, or one teacher may lecture while the other models note-taking strategies.

According to Salend (1994) co-teaching typically occurs for a set period of time on certain days of the week or every day. A group of students with disabilities who used to attend a separate class for a specific subject will join a general education class permanently. In effect, there is a special class within a general class, a quarter to a half of whom may be at risk or have disabilities. Another strategy for co-teaching is to have the special education and general education teachers share instruction for a particular unit.

Multiple variations of approaches of the co-teaching model exist. In one approach, one teacher leads the lesson and the other takes an assisting role. For instance, while the special education teacher leads a lesson on comprehension strategies, the classroom teacher gathers observational data. Alternatively, while the classroom teacher leads a lesson on the Revolutionary War, the special education teacher keeps students on task, checks written work as it is being completed, and responds quietly to student questions. Or supportive learning activities may be developed by the special educator to supplement the content delivered by the general education teacher (Thomas, Correa, & Morsink, 1995).

Friend and Bursuck (1996) describe three new models of instruction to mainstream classes: station teaching, parallel teaching, and alternative teaching. During station teaching, particularly found in kindergarten classes, curricular content is divided into two parts. One teacher teaches part of the content to half of the students while the other teaches the other part to the rest. Then the groups rotate and each teacher reiterates her part of the lesson. A third group can be constructed with "learning buddies" who tutor each other on assignments. An entire lesson based on stations can be completed in a single day in an elementary school, while in secondary schools, students might take a class period or more.

When it becomes advantageous to divide a heterogeneous class in half, and have each teacher instruct the class separately, co-teaching takes on a parallel-teaching format. In an elementary school, this approach might be used to enable students to read different books based on their interests. Or teachers particularly skilled in presenting information one way could be matched with students who learn best when instructed with that approach.

Alternative teaching occurs when it is appropriate to divide the class into groups, one large and one small. Traditionally, the small group has been used primarily for remediation, but many other options are possible. For example, some students may benefit from preteaching where they get a "head start" on learning, reviewing or receiving additional practice on a particular concept, or even extending activities such as enrichment. Small-group membership varies depending on the concept taught and particular needs of the children. This type of co-teaching provides opportunities for small-group instruction that is more explicit, closely monitored, and more strategic.

Sindelar (1995) states: "There seem to be about as many different ways for teachers to collaborate as there are pairs of teachers collaborating, and individual teachers may take on many different roles in their various collaborations with their colleagues" (p. 239). Although we are well aware of the importance of equality in partnerships, little can be inferred from the research about how best to collaborate during planning or instruction. We need to know with greater certainty what to teach our preservice students about working with one another, and we need to learn what benefits can be realized from implementing various models of co-teaching.

Many educators assert that models such as the ones described above will benefit general and special educators as well as their students with disabilities. For students, collaborative models will reduce the stigma attached to pull-out and labeling, will decrease the disruption of instruction caused by leaving one setting to receive services in another, will provide positive role models, and will promote independence. For teachers, collaborative approaches will reduce the rate of unwarranted referrals, will allow mutual sharing of knowledge, will improve attitudes toward students with disabilities, and will improve communication between general and special education teachers (Smith et al., 1995).

We need to learn how to move teachers toward one another for the purpose of working on common problems, and we also need to learn how to do the same with our organizations. When we consider the organizational structure of teacher education programs and the needs of diverse groups of children who attend our nation's schools, we find a need to train teachers as general practitioners and as specialists. General practitioners serve students who are able to function in large-group situations, and who are usually capable of learning regardless of the instructional approach. Specialists must be able to choose explicit types of instruction; they must teach compensatory skills and help students apply such skills in mainstreamed settings. They must determine why mainstreamed students are not learning in the regular classroom at a rate commensurate with their abilities and assess whether students have mastered some part of the curriculum. If generalists and specialists are to cooperate on such matters, they need a common perspective on the educational world.

A collaborative or co-teaching approach will require more dialogue, planning, and coordination between teacher educators in both general education and special education than presently exists. Special educators and regular educators should work with one another in staff meetings and on committee assignments. Faculty members should be sent in teams to each other's conferences. Open communication should be encouraged, and team teaching should be supported by administrators. Participants must be assured they will not lose face by not knowing, and will not be embarrassed by becoming learners again.

Rorty's (1991) observations on communication within a diverse community are instructive. Referring to anthropologist Clifford Geertz's metaphor of a Kuwaiti bazaar, Rorty writes:

> I picture many of the people in such a bazaar as preferring to die rather than share the beliefs of many of those with whom they are haggling, yet as haggling profitably away nevertheless . . . But you can have a civil society of the bourgeois democratic sort. All you need is the ability to control your feelings when people who strike you as irredeemably different show up at City Hall, or the greengrocers, or the bazaar. When this happens, you smile a lot, make the best deals you can, and, after a hard day's haggling, retreat to your club. There you will be comforted by the companionship of your moral equals. (p. 209)

Perhaps we, too, can haggle over mainstreaming, pull-out programs, the existence of learning disabilities, and the administrative and economic imperatives to make such programs work without feeling compelled to impose uniformity of action. Intense debate with the opposition need not cause people to abandon their ideals or allegiance to locally defined programs that have practical advantages. We could still seek what Rorty (1991) calls "solidarity" with the community of researchers, practitioners, parents, and students who desire to make education for all students the best it can be.

There are several immediate steps teacher educators might take to encourage solidarity. If general and special education teachers are going to work together in education programs, they ought to have experiences working together in classes and field experiences as teacher education students (Sindelar, 1995). Students might first take coursework to develop special expertise in their own areas and later incorporate other knowledge and skills needed to work in collaborative situations as generalists and specialists. With some forethought, courses can emerge that begin to bring the two groups together.

A combination of consultation and direct services appears to provide effective instructional strategies for student achievement (Schulte, Osborne, & McKinney, 1990). So the optimal university programs would train learning disabilities specialists in both a collaborative-consultative model and a diagnostic-prescriptive model. Special education preservice teachers could be exposed to direct instruction, curriculum adaptation, learning strategies, and study skills instruction. Separate coursework for regular education preservice teachers could focus on models of teaching that emphasize the acquisition of information, personal development, and social inquiry.

Courses that combine regular education and special education content might follow where students would be separated or combined. In these courses, content from previously taught courses could be presented in a parallel manner so that both groups would begin to understand the relationships between special and regular educators that facilitate teaching mainstreamed students. Courses in information-processing strategies come immediately to mind, as well as those in behavior management. Even though such courses might be taught separately, special and regular education faculty members could plan content cooperatively.

Courses could be offered by teams of special educators and regular educators. In these courses, preservice teachers could be helped to synthesize what they have learned in previous courses, that is, to examine their thinking and behavior with respect to particular problem situations. They could explore concepts such as cooperative planning, teaching teams, and teacher assistance teams. Case studies, simulations of problem-solving strategies, and role reversals could be major components of such courses so neophytes could practice their actions in low-stakes situations instead of practicing on real children in real schools.

Upon reaching their field placements, all prospective teachers, regardless of their area of concentration, could be required to analyze the problems of students with disabilities who are mainstreamed and to design collaborative interventions with administrative interns working in the same schools. Currently, teachers and school administrators never even see each other until they cross the threshold at their first place of employment. Bringing together aspiring professionals early and often should reinforce the need to focus human and material resources to promote student welfare.

It is not until prospective teachers work in the schools with typical students and students with mild disabilities that teachers will be put to the test. To create a school environment appropriate for such a test will require close cooperation or a "tighter coupling" between in-service teachers and school administrators—a condition that heretofore has been uncommon (Cuban, 1990).

Schools can take some simple but direct actions. They can encourage collaboration between in-service teachers, teacher educators, prospective teachers, and school administrators. Most notably, people can be given opportunities to engage in active, consistent communication with one another about issues of teaching and learning, particularly with respect to the needs of especially demanding students. General and special education teachers can plan their programs together. Consultants can be advisors, not supervisors; and they can use a combination of expert and collaborative approaches to shape teams of professionals to help children. General and special education teachers can seek instructional materials and methods that will best fit their students and their objectives, and they can be helped to articulate publicly the reasons for these decisions. School and university representatives can collaborate to articulate definitions of successful learning and teaching that will accord with professional experience and make practical sense to the public as well.

The sociopolitical dimensions of mainstreaming argue for a "mixture of unforced agreement with tolerant disagreement" (Rorty, 1991, p. 43). If we can help each other think about what we do and why, and compare our actions with the actions of others who are successful, then we shall have begun to move toward useful development across the professional spectrum.

We cannot depend solely on the good sense of a program to improve the lives of all students. Nor can we rely on the promise of new and better achievement tests that will yield data upon which to base new and better programs, regardless of how authentic those data may be. Instead, we must reach out in print and in action to involve others in designing, implementing, and judging educational programs for both teachers and students. In short, we educators must do all in our power to seek the popular feeling that exists in society for helping children who need help.

Some Effective Teachers' Actions

1. Teachers watch students as they work on tasks:
   (a) to see if students need help.
   (b) to keep students involved.
   (c) to determine when to move on to the next activity.

2. Teachers give step-by-step directions:
   (a) to help students work independently.
   (b) to avoid interruptions during instructional time.

3. Teachers help learners by giving hints and clarifying misunderstandings:
   (a) to make the content of a lesson more meaningful.
   (b) to help students make connections between old and new material.
   (c) to get students to think.
   (d) to keep students from giving up.
   (e) to give students more time to think.
   (f) to help students succeed so they feel good about themselves.

4. Teachers recognize special needs of learners:*
   (a) to give students concrete examples to help them understand.

5. Teachers summarize and review throughout the lesson:
   (a) to help students synthesize information.
   (b) to keep students involved.

*These behaviors are not always easily observed. It is often necessary to elicit the teacher's thoughts before behaviors become apparent.

6. Teachers praise learners publicly and explain why:
   (a) to encourage student involvement.
   (b) to make students feel good about their achievements.
   (c) to encourage students to behave like others.
   (d) to enhance self-concepts of students.

7. Teachers make connections to students' interests, to the outside world, and to other subjects:
   (a) to increase student attention and interest in the lesson.
   (b) to make content real or meaningful to students.
   (c) to help students see that there is an overlap in content areas.
   (d) to help students form linkages between subjects.
   (e) to reinforce what the teacher and class have just discussed.

8. Teachers urge students to answer/comment:
   (a) to get and keep student involvement.
   (b) to get students to think about the material.
   (c) to give students a chance to answer correctly and feel good about themselves.
   (d) to make students feel that what they have to say is important.

9. Teachers check understanding throughout the lesson:
   (a) to see if students are "with" the teacher.
   (b) to keep students involved in the lesson.
   (c) to get students to think on their own.

10. Teachers question and respond—they praise, acknowledge, approve, redirect, re-enter, make eye contact, check status, and so on:
    (a) to keep students involved in the lesson.
    (b) to check understanding.
    (c) to get students to think.
    (d) to review concepts.

11. Teachers work to build students' self-concepts:*
    (a) to help students feel that what they have to say is important.
    (b) to help students develop a feeling of power or control—a "can do" attitude.
    (c) to increase student participation.

References

Ahlgren, A. (1983). *Minnesota school attitude survey: Manual.* Chicago: Science Research Associates.

Argyris, C., & Schön, D. A. (1974). *Theory in practice: Increasing professional effectiveness.* San Francisco: Jossey-Bass.

Baird, J. R., Fensham, P. J., Gunstone, R. F., Penna, C., & White, R. T. (1991, April). *Challenge: A focus for improving teaching and learning.* Paper presented at the annual meeting of the American Educational Research Association, Chicago.

Bennett, N. (1976). *Teaching styles and pupil progress.* Cambridge, MA: Harvard University Press.

Berliner, D. C. (1990). If the metaphor fits, why not wear it? The teacher as executive. *Theory Into Practice, 29,* 85-93.

Brock, T. C. (1967). Communication discrepancy and intent to persuade as determinants of counterargument production. *Journal of Experimental Social Psychology, 2,* 269-309.

Brophy, J., & Good, T. L. (1986). Teacher behavior and student achievement. In M. C. Wittrock (Ed.), *Handbook of research on teaching* (3rd ed., pp. 328-375). New York: Macmillan.

Bruner, J. (1996). *The culture of education.* Cambridge, MA: Harvard University Press.

Cacioppo, J. T., & Petty, R. E. (1981). Social psychological procedures for cognitive response assessment: The thought listing technique. In T. V. Merluzzi, C. R. Glass, & M. Genest (Eds.), *Cognitive assessment* (pp. 309-342). New York: Guilford Press.

Calderhead, J. (1981). Stimulated recall: A method for research on teaching. *British Journal of Educational Psychology, 51,* 211-217.

Calderhead, J. (1996). Teachers: Beliefs and knowledge. In D. C. Berliner & R. C. Calfee (Eds.), *Handbook of educational psychology* (pp. 709-725). New York: Simon & Schuster Macmillan.

Clandinin, D. J. (1985). Personal practical knowledge: A study of teachers' classroom images. *Curriculum Inquiry, 15* (4), 361-385.

Clark, C. M., & Peterson, P. L. (1986). Teachers' thought processes. In M.C. Wittrock (Ed.), *Handbook of research on teaching*(3rd ed., pp. 255-296). New York: Macmillan.

Cohen, E. G., & Lotan, R. A. (1990). Teacher as supervisor of complex technology. *Theory into Practice, 29,* 78-84.

Connelly, F. M., & Clandinin, D. J. (1985). Personal practical knowledge and the modes of knowing: Relevance for teaching and learning. In E. Eisner (Ed.), *Learning and teaching the ways of knowing* (National Society for Studies in Education Yearbook, pp. 174-198). Chicago: University of Chicago Press.

Connelly, F. M., & Clandinin, D. J. (1988). *Teachers as curriculum planners: Narratives of experience.* New York: Teachers College Press.

Cuban, L. (1990). Reforming again, again, and again. *Educational Researcher, 19* (1), 3-13.

Darling-Hammond, L., Wise, A., & Pease, S. (1983). Teacher evaluation in the organizational context: A review of the literature. *Review of Educational Research, 53* (3), 285-328.

Dewalt, M. W. (1986, August). *The effects of teacher training on teacher competency.* Unpublished doctoral dissertation, University of Virginia.

Dewey, J. (1904). The relation of theory to practice in education. In C.A. McMurry (Ed.), *The relation of theory to practice in the education of teachers* (Third Yearbook of the National Society for the Scientific Study of Education, Part I, pp. 9-30). Chicago: University of Chicago Press.

Dewey, J. (1933). *How we think: A restatement of the relation of reflective thinking to the educative process.* Boston: D.C. Heath.

Doss, A. R. (1987, May). *Investigation of teaching behaviors.* Unpublished doctoral dissertation, University of Virginia.

Elbaz, F. (1983). *Teacher thinking: A case study of practical knowledge.* London: Croom Helm.

Erickson, F. (1986). Qualitative methods in research on teaching. In M.C. Wittrock (Ed.), *Handbook of research on teaching.* (3rd ed., pp. 119-161). New York: Macmillan.

Erlandson, D. A., Harris, E. L., Skipper, B. L., & Allen, S. D. (1993). *Doing naturalistic inquiry: A guide to methods.* Newbury Park, CA: Sage.

Fenstermacher, G. D. (1978). A philosophical consideration of recent research on teacher effectiveness. In L. S. Shulman (Ed.), *Review of research in education* (Vol. 6, pp. 122-147. Itasca, IL F. E.Peacock.

Friend, M., & Bursuck, W. D. (1996). *Including students with special needs: A practical guide for classroom teachers.* Needham Heights, MA: Allyn & Bacon.

Gage, N. L. (1978). *The scientific basis of the art of teaching.* New York: Teachers College Press.

Gage, N. L. (1985). *Hard gains in the soft sciences: The case of pedagogy.* Bloomington, IN: Phi Delta Kappa's Center on Evaluation, Development, and Research.

Gage, N.L., & Needels, M.C. (1989). Process-product research on teaching: A review of criticisms. *The Elementary School Journal, 89* (3), 253-300.

Gearheart, B. R., Weishahn, M. W., & Gearheart, C. J. (1996). *The exceptional student in the regular classroom.* Englewood Cliffs, NJ: Prentice Hall.

Geertz, C. (1973) *Interpretation of cultures.* New York: Basic Books.

Good, T. L., & Brophy, J. E. (1994). *Looking in classrooms* (6th ed.). New York: Harper & Row.

Goodman, N. (1982). The way the world is. In E. Bredo & W. Feinberg (Eds.), *Knowledge and values in social and educational research,* (pp. 129-136) Philadelphia: Temple University Press.

Goodman, N., and Elgin, C. Z. (1988). *Reconceptions in philosophy and other arts and sciences.* London: Routledge.

Greenwald, A. G. (1968). Cognitive learning, cognitive response to persuasion, and attitude change. In A. G. Greenwald, T. C. Brock, & T. M. Ostrom (Eds.), *Psychological foundations of attitudes.* New York: Academic Press.

Hallahan, D. P., Kauffman, J. M., & Lloyd, J. W. (1996). *Introduction to learning disabilities* (2nd ed.). Needham Heights, MA: Allyn & Bacon.

Hallahan, D. P., Lloyd, J. W., & Stoller, L. (1982). *Improving attention with self-monitoring: A manual for teachers.* Charlottesville: University of Virginia, Learning Disabilities Research Institute.

Hallahan, D. P., McNergney, R. F., & McKinney, J. D. (1986). *Improving teaching effectiveness with learning-disabled mainstreamed students.* Charlottesville, VA : U. S. Department of Education, Office of Special Education and Rehabilitative Services, University of Virginia. Grant No. G008630227.

Hallahan, D. P., McNergney, R. F., & McKinney, J. D. (1989*). Final report: Improving teacher effectiveness with learning-disabled mainstreamed students.* Charlottesville, VA: Office of Special Education and

Rehabilitative Services, U. S. Department of Education, Grant No. G008630227. University of Virginia.

Harris, F. C., & Lahey, B. B. (1978). A method for combining occurrence and nonoccurrence interobserver agreement scores. *Journal of Applied Behavior Analysis, 11* (4), 523-527.

Herbert, J., & Keller, C. (1989, April). *A case study of an effective teacher in an inner-city mainstreamed classroom*. Paper presented at the annual meeting of the American Educational Research Association, San Francisco.

Herbert, J. M. (1990). *Encouraging teachers of mainstreamed students to use effective teaching strategies*. Unpublished doctoral dissertation, University of Virginia.

Herbert, J. M., & Tankersley, M. (1993). More and less effective ways to intervene with classroom teachers. *Journal of Curriculum and Supervision, 9*(1), 24-40.

Herbert, J.M., & McNergney, R.F. (1995). *Guide to foundations in action videocases: Teaching and learning in multicultural settings*. Boston, MA: Allyn & Bacon.

Howey, K. R., & Zimpher, N. L. (1996). Patterns in prospective teachers: Guides for designing preservice programs. In F. B. Murray (Ed.), *The teacher educator's handbook: Building a knowledge base for the preparation of teachers* (pp. 465-505). San Francisco: Jossey-Bass.

Hunt, D.E. (1971). *Matching models in education*. Monograph series No. 10. Toronto: Ontario Institute for Studies in Education.

Hunt, D. E. (1987). *Beginning with ourselves: In practice, theory, and human affairs*. Cambridge, MA.: Brookline Books, and Toronto: Ontario Institute for Studies in Education Press.

Jackson, P. W. (1968). *Life in classrooms*. New York: Holt, Rinehart, & Winston.

Joyce, B., & Weil, M. (1972). *Models of teaching*. Englewood Cliffs, NJ: Prentice Hall.

Kauffman, J. M. (1989). The Regular Education Initiative as Reagan-Bush education policy: A trickle-down theory of education of the hard-to-teach. *Journal of Special Education, 23,* 256-278.

Kauffman, J. M., Gerber, M. M., & Semmel, M. I. (1988). Arguable assumptions underlying the Regular Education Initiative. *Journal of Learning Disabilities, 21,* 6-11.

Kauffman, J. M., & Pullen, P. L. (1989). A personal perspective on our history of service to mildly handicapped and at risk students. *Remedial and Special Education, 10* (6), 12-14.

Keller, C. E., McKinney, J. D., & Hallahan, D. P. (1990). *Comparisons between beginning general and special education teachers' instructional behaviors at three grade levels.* Unpublished manuscript.

Kennedy, M. M. (1990). Choosing a goal for professional education. In W.R. Houston (Ed.), *Handbook of research on teacher education* (pp. 813-825). New York: Macmillan Library Reference.

Kennedy, M. M. (1991, Spring). *An agenda for research on teacher learning.* East Lansing, MI:Michigan State University, National Center for Research on Teacher Learning.

Kleinfeld, J. (1992). Learning to think like a teacher: The study of cases. In J.H. Shulman (Ed.), *Case methods in teacher education* (pp. 33-49). New York: Teachers College Press.

Lakoff, G., & Johnson, M. (1980). *Metaphors we live by.* Chicago: University of Chicago Press.

Larrivee, B. (1985). *Effective teaching for successful mainstreaming.* New York: Longman.

Lepper, M. R. (1983). Extrinsic reward and intrinsic motivation. In J. Levine & M. C. Wang (Eds.), *Teacher and student perceptions: Implications for learning.* Hillsdale, NJ: Lawrence Erlbaum.

Lincoln, Y. S., & Guba, E. G. (1985). *Naturalistic inquiry.* Beverly Hills, CA: Sage.

Lippmann, W. (1913). *A preface to politics.* New York: M. Kennerley.

Lloyd, J. W., & Landrum, T. J. (1990). Self-recording of attending to task: Treatment components and generalization of effects. In T. E. Scruggs & B. Y. L. Wong (Eds.), *Intervention research in learning disabilities* (pp. 235-262). New York: Springer-Verlag.

McKinney, J. D. (1987). *Methodological studies of the classroom performance record* (Report for Grant No. G008630227). Unpublished manuscript. University of North Carolina at Chapel Hill, Frank Porter Graham Child Development Center.

McKinney, J. D. (1988). Research in conceptually and empirically derived subtypes of specific learning disabilities. In M. Wang, M. Reynolds, & H. Walberg (Eds.), *Handbook of special education: Research and practice: Vol. 2. Mildly handicapping conditions* (pp. 253-281). Oxford, England: Pergamon Press.

McKinney, J. D., & Hocutt, A. M. (1988). Policy issues in the evaluation of the Regular Education Initiative. *Learning Disabilities Focus, 4,* 15–234.

McNergney, R. F., & Carrier, C. A. (1981). *Teacher development.* New York: Macmillan.

McNergney, R., Hallahan, D., & Sutton, J. (1989, April). *Teacher thinking and behavior in mainstreamed classrooms*. Paper presented at the annual meeting of the American Educational Research Association, San Francisco.

McNergney, R.F., Herbert J.M., & Ford R.E. (1993, April). *Anatomy of a team case competition*. Paper presented at the annual meeting of the American Educational Research Association, Atlanta, Georgia.

McNergney, R.F., Herbert J.M., & Ford R.E. (1994). Cooperation and competition in case-based teacher education. *Journal of Teacher Education, 45* (5), 339-345.

McNergney, R.F., & Herbert, J.M. (1998). *Foundations of education: The challenge of professional practice* (2nd ed.). Boston, MA: Allyn & Bacon.

McNergney, R., Medley, D., & Caldwell, M. (1988). *Guide to classroom teaching*. Boston: Allyn & Bacon.

McShane, E., & Cox, C. (1989, April*). A case study of an effective teacher in a rural mainstreamed classroom*. Paper presented at the annual meeting of the American Educational Research Association, San Francisco.

Medley, D. M. (1977). *Teacher competence and teacher effectiveness: A review of process-product research*. Washington: American Association of Colleges for Teacher Education.

Medley, D. M., Rosenblum, E. P., & Vance, N. C. (1989). Assessing the functional knowledge of participants in the Virginia Beginning Teacher Assistance Program. *Elementary School Journal, 89 (*4), 481-496.

Merseth, K.K. (1991). The early history of case-based instruction: Insights for teacher education today. *Journal of Teacher Education, 42* (4), 243-249.

Merseth, K.K. (1996). Cases and case methods in teacher education. In J. Sikula, T. Buttery, & E. Guyton (Eds.), *Handbook of research on teacher education* (pp. 722-744). New York: Macmillan Library Reference.

Mitzel, H. (1960). Teacher effectiveness. In C. W. Harris (Ed.), *Encyclopedia of educational research* (3rd. ed., pp. 1481-1486). New York: Macmillan.

Morine-Dershimer, G. (1979). *Teachers' conceptions of pupils—an outgrowth of instructional context: The South Bay study, Part III*. East Lansing: Michigan State University, Institute for Research on Teaching.

Morine-Dershimer, G. (1982). *Pupil perceptions of teacher praise*. Washington: ERIC Clearinghouse on Teacher Education. (ERIC Document Reproduction Service No. EJ 264 935)

Morine-Dershimer, G. (1983). *Tapping teacher thinking through triangulation of data sets*. Austin, TX: Research and Development Center for Teacher Education.

Morine-Dershimer, G. (1984, April). *Complexity and imagery in teacher thought: Alternative analyses of stimulated recall data.* Paper presented at the meeting of the American Educational Research Association, New Orleans.

Munby, H. (1986). Metaphor in the thinking of teachers: An exploratory study. *Journal of Curriculum Studies, 18,* 197-209.

Munby, H., & Russell, T. (1990). Metaphor in the study of teachers' professional knowledge. *Theory into Practice, 29,* 116-121.

National Association of State Boards of Education, (1995). *Winning ways: Creating inclusive schools, classrooms, and communities.* Alexandria, VA: Author.

Nowacek, E. J., McKinney, J. D., & Hallahan, D. P. (1990). Instructional behaviors of more and less effective beginning regular and special educators. *Exceptional Children, 57,* 140-149.

Nowacek, E. J., & Saunders, S. (1989). *A case study of an effective teacher in a suburban mainstreamed classroom.* Paper presented at the annual meeting of the American Education Research Association, San Francisco.

Peterson, P.L. (1989). Alternatives to student retention: New images of the learner, the teacher, and classroom learning. In L.A. Shepard & M.L. Smith (Eds.), *Flunking grades: Research and policies on retention* (pp. 174-201). Philadelphia: The Falmer Press.

Peterson, P.L., & Swing, S.R. (1982). Beyond time on task: Students' reports of their thought processes during classroom instruction. *Elementary School Journal, 82* (5), 481-491.

Peterson, P. L. (1988). Teachers' and students' cognitional knowledge for classroom teaching and learning. *Educational Researcher, 17* (5), 5-14.

Polanyi, M. (1964). *Personal knowledge: Towards a post-critical philosophy.* New York: Harper & Row.

Provenzo, E. F., McCloskey, G. N., Kottkamp, R. B., & Cohn, M. M. (1989). Metaphor and meaning in the language of teachers. *Teachers College Record, 90,* 551-573.

Reynolds, M. C. (1989). An historical perspective: The delivery of special education to mildly disabled and at-risk students. *Remedial and Special Education, 10* (6), 7-11.

Risko, V. (1991). Videodisc-based case methodology: A design for enhancing preservice teachers' problem-solving abilities. *American Reading Forum, 11,* 121-137. (ERIC Document Reproduction No. ED 340 002)

Rorty, R. (1991). *Objectivity, relativism, and truth.* New York: Cambridge University Press.

Rosenshine, B. (1983). Teaching functions in instructional programs. *Elementary School Journal, 83* (4), 335-354.

Russell, T., Munby, H., Spafford, C., & Johnston, P. (1988). Learning the professional knowledge of teaching: Metaphors, puzzles, and the theory-practice relationship. In P. P. Grimmett and G. Erickson (Eds.) *Reflection in teacher education* (pp. 67-89). New York: Teachers College Press.

Salend, S. J. (1994). *Effective mainstreaming: Creating inclusive classrooms* (2nd ed.). New York: Macmillan.

Salend, S. J., Brooks, L., & Salend, S. (1987). Identifying school districts' policies for implementing mainstreaming. *The Pointer, 32*, 34-37.

Salomon, G. (1981). *Communication and education: Social and psychological interactions.* Beverly Hills, CA: Sage.

Sapon-Shevin, M. (1988). Working towards merger together: Seeing beyond distrust and fear. *Teacher Education and Special Education, 11* (3), 103-110.

Scardamalia, M., & Bereiter, C. (1996). Computer support for knowledge-building communities. In T. Koschmann (Ed.), *CSCL: Theory and practice of an emerging paradigm.* Mahwah, NJ: Lawrence Erlbaum Associates.

Schön, D. A. (1979). Generative metaphor: A perspective on problem–setting in social policy. In A. Ortony (Ed.), *Metaphor and thought* (pp. 254-283). Cambridge, England: Cambridge University Press.

Schulte, A. C., Osborne, S. S., & McKinney, J. D. (1990). Academic outcomes for students with learning disabilities in consultation and resource programs. *Exceptional Children, 57*, 162-172.

Shulman, J. (1986). Paradigms and research programs in the study of teaching. In M. C. Wittrock (Ed.), *Handbook of research on teaching* (3rd ed., pp. 3-36). New York: Macmillan.

Shulman, L.S. (1992). Toward a pedagogy of cases. In J. Shulman (Ed.), *Case methods in teacher education* (pp. 1-30). New York: Teachers College Press, 1-30.

Sindelar, P. T. (1995). Full inclusion of students with learning disabilities and its implications for teacher education. *Journal of Special Education, 29*, 234-244.

Smith, T. E. C., Polloway, E. A., Patton, J. R., & Dowdy, C. A. (1995). *Teaching students with special needs in inclusive settings.* Needham Heights, MA: Allyn & Bacon.

Sprinthall, N. A., & Thies-Sprinthall, L. (1987). Experienced teachers: Agents for revitalization and renewal as mentors and teacher educators. *Journal of Education, 169* (1), 65-79.

Sprinthall, N.A., & Thies-Sprinthall, L. (1983). The teacher as adult learner: A cognitive-developmental view. *National Society for the Study of Education Yearbook*, (Pt. 2), 13-35.

Stainback, S., & Stainback, W. (1985). The merger of special and regular education: Can it be done? A response to Lieberman and Mesinger. *Exceptional Children, 51*, 517-521.

Stainback, S., & Stainback, W. (1987). Facilitating merger through personnel preparation. *Teacher Education and Special Education, 10,* 185-190.

Sutton, J. P. (1989). *The effects of grade level and program type on teachers' instructional behaviors in learning disabilities classrooms.* Unpublished doctoral dissertation, University of Virginia.

Sudzina, M., & Kilbane, C. (1992). Applications of a case study text to undergraduate teacher preparation. In Hans Klein (Ed.), *Forging new partnerships with cases, simulations, games and other interactive methods.* Needham, MA: WACRA.

Tate, P. M. (1991). *State-level policy making for teacher education: A four state case study of changes in curriculum standards.* Unpublished doctoral dissertation, University of Chicago.

Thomas, C. C., Correa, V. I., Morsink, C. V. (1995). *Interactive teaming: Consultation and collaboration in special programs.* Englewood Cliffs, NJ: Prentice Hall.

Tobin, K. (1990). Changing metaphors and beliefs: A master switch for teaching? *Theory into Practice, 29*, 122-127.

Trent, S. (1989). Much to do about nothing: A clarification of issues on the Regular Education Initiative. *Journal of Learning Disabilities, 22*, 23-25,45.

University of Virginia. (1987). *Virginia Beginning Teacher Assistance Program: Beginning teacher orientation handbook.* Charlottesville, VA: Author.

Walberg, H. J. (1984). Improving the productivity of America's schools. *Educational Leadership, 41*(8), 19-30.

Will, M. C. (1986*). Educating children with learning problems: A shared responsibility.* A report to the secretary. Washington, DC: U.S. Department of Education.

Wise, A., Darling-Hammond, L., McLaughlin, M., & Bernstein, H. (1984). *Teacher evaluation: A study of effective practices.* Santa Monica, CA: Rand.

Yin, R. K. (1984). *Case study research: Design and methods.* Beverly Hills, CA: Sage.

Yinger, R. J., & Clark, C. M. (1981, July). *Reflective journal writing: Theory and practice* (Occasional Paper No. 50). East Lansing, MI: Michigan State University, Institute for Research on Teaching.

Yinger, R. J., & Clark, C. M. (1985, February*). Using personal documents to study teacher thinking* (Occasional Paper No. 84). East Lansing: Michigan State University, Institute for Research on Teaching.

Zigler, E. (1987, August). *From theory to practice.* The Edgar A. Doll address given at the annual meeting of the American Psychological Association

Zigmond, N., Jenkins, J., Fuchs, L., Deno, S., Fuchs, D., Baker, J., Jenkins, L., & Couthino, M. (1995). Special education in restructured schools: Findings from three multi-year studies. *Phi Delta Kappan, 76,* 531-540.

Index

Source Books on Education

RELIGIOUS HIGHER EDUCATION
IN THE UNITED STATES
A Source Book
edited by Thomas C. Hunt
and James C. Carper

MULTICULTURALISM IN
ACADEME
A Source Book
by Libby V. Morris
and Sammy Parker

TEACHERS AND MENTORS
*Profiles of Distinguished
Twentieth-Century Professors
of Education*
edited by Craig Kridel,
Robert V. Bullough, Jr.,
and Paul Shaker

AT-RISK YOUTH
Theory, Practice, Reform
by Robert F. Kronick

RELIGION AND SCHOOLING
IN CONTEMPORARY AMERICA
*Confronting Our
Cultural Pluralism*
edited by Thomas C. Hunt
and James C. Carper

CHILDREN'S LITERATURE
Developing Good Readers
edited by Hannah Nuba,
Deborah Lovitky Sheiman,
and Michael Searson

K–12 CASE STUDIES
FOR SCHOOL ADMINISTRATORS
Problems, Issues, and Resources
by Marcia M. Norton
and Paula E. Lester

IMAGES OF MAINSTREAMING
Educating Students with Disabilities
edited by Robert McNergney
and Clayton Keller

MULTICULTURAL EDUCATION
A Source Book
by Patricia G. Ramsey,
Edwina Battle Vold,
and Leslie R. Williams